MAKE MORE MONEY, FIND MORE CLIENTS, CLOSE DEALS FASTER

THE CANADIAN REAL ESTATE AGENT'S ESSENTIAL BUSINESS GUIDE

by Claude Boiron

WILEY

Wiley publishes in a variety of print and electronic formats and by print-on-demand. Some material included with standard print versions of this book may not be included in e-books or in print-on-demand. For more information about Wiley products, visit www.wiley.com.

For general information about our other products and services, please contact our Customer Care Department within the United States at (800) 762–2974, outside the United States at (317) 572–3993, or fax (317) 572–4002.

Library and Archives Canada Cataloguing in Publication Data
Boiron, Claude
    Make more money, find more clients, close deals faster : the Canadian real estate agent's essential business guide / Claude Boiron.

Includes index.
ISBN 978-1-118-00804-1 (pbk); 978-1-118-01878-1 (ebk); 978-1-118-01879-8 (ebk); 978-1-118-01880-4 (ebk)

    1. Real estate business—Canada. 2. Real estate agents—Canada. I. Title.

HD1375.B67 2013   333.330971   C2013-900198-0

Production Credits
Cover design: Ian Koo
Cover photo: Hemera/Thinkstock
Managing Editor: Alison Maclean
Production Editor: Lindsay Humphreys
Composition: Thomson Digital
Printer: Friesens Corporation

John Wiley & Sons Canada, Ltd.
6045 Freemont Blvd.
Mississauga, Ontario
L5R 4J3

Printed in Canada

1 2 3 4 5 FP 17 16 15 14 13

To Belle, who makes her papa proud and brings him joy daily.

And to Anja, a transcendent beauty whose spirit and joie de vivre shine with a light so bright, she is the companion of my dreams. Volim te.

This book would not have been possible without my own mentor and father, Pierre. Thank you for teaching me all I know about real estate.

Table of Contents

Foreword

*by Andrew Zsolt, Owner & Broker of Record
(Coldwell Banker Terrequity Realty)*

If you're an aspiring realtor or one that has just been licensed, do you really understand the profession that you have gotten yourself into? As a consumer, have you ever wondered what your agent is doing for you? What should she be doing for you? How does a good realtor earn his commission? Where does all that money go?

In his easy-to-read writing style, with numerous fascinating examples, Claude Boiron affords the reader an insider's look at how realtors think and act, and how they should be thinking and acting for the ultimate good of their clients and themselves.

Due to the way real estate licensing is structured in most of Canada, many realtors do have a good idea of how to fill out forms and how to avoid being fined or sued. Of course they understand the steps they need to take to remain licensed. Unfortunately, however, many don't receive the appropriate education about business, marketing and advertising (of themselves or their clients' listings), negotiations, deal-making strategy, and so on.

Having known Claude for more than a decade, and being familiar with his extensive training programs at several universities, I can say that Claude is a unique combination of entrepreneur, caring salesperson, and knowledgeable realtor. If you are interested in a career in real estate, want to improve your knowledge as a practising realtor, or are simply passionate about real estate and want to take a peek behind the curtain to see how the real estate industry operates, I urge you to read this book.

Acknowledgements

This book benefited greatly from the help of several people who read through the manuscript and provided comments, supplementary stories, and material: Abcar Ohanessian, Paul Grissom, and James Basnett (Toronto Realtor Media). For contributions to the chapter on advertising and marketing: Crystal DeVries, Joe Almeida, Christiane Yerex, Rita Pardatscher, Anja Perendija, and Pierre Boiron. I would also like to thank the various contributors of material and stories in the Tales from the Trenches part of this book, including Heather Holmes, Farrell Macdonald, Joanna Duong, Andrew Wells, Paul Gill, Shawn Bedard, Gerald Moodie, and Maciek Tarnowski.

PART

I

The Business of Real Estate

Is Real Estate for You?

I'm a realtor.

I absolutely love what I do for a living. There are very few professions where you can be a combination of entrepreneur, salesperson, friend, adviser, negotiator, and dealmaker, and also be able to draft contracts, while having the freedom to create your own schedule and the potential to earn a substantial income. If you bring the right attitude and discipline to the table, even if you are not a natural salesperson, the job of being a realtor can provide a great deal more for you than you can imagine—both financially and in terms of lifestyle.

I don't believe in mincing words, so I'm blunt from the beginning of this guide to the end. My hope is that this book enables realtors to think about how they can improve in their career, be motivated to aim higher, and earn more money. At the same time, I also hope that some who read this book realize that selling real estate is not what they truly want to do. This reality check is better not only for them personally in the long run, but also for the industry as a whole. As in any profession, those who are not as professional and motivated as the rest can have a deleterious effect on the whole.

The real estate brokerage industry in Canada is in trouble, and has been for a very long time. There are three reasons that I make this statement. First, the general public perceives realty as a profession to be only a notch above politicians and used-car salesmen when it comes to values such as honesty and integrity. Increasingly, consumers are becoming polarized regarding realtors. Some people believe we're practically worth our weight in gold (and some of us are!). However, others think: "I'm just as smart, or smarter, than any realtor. I'm quite capable of putting a sign on my lawn to let people know my house is for sale. And now that the Multiple Listing Service (MLS) is open to the public, I can list my property on MLS. How hard can it be to arrange and host an open house? Put out some coffee and tea and a few doughnuts—what's the big deal? I know my property better than anyone, so I can present it in the best possible light. And I'm going to keep thousands of dollars I'd otherwise be paying in commissions." How is it that our profession has failed to inspire confidence and standards in the public we serve? This must change.

Second, because most people who have some degree of literacy can take the necessary courses and pass the certification exams to become a realtor and broker, it is not too much of a challenge to start one's own brokerage. In my view, there are many brokerage owners who should not be running a brokerage. They lack business skills and training. They don't understand that they need to offer quality services and support to realtors in order to attract effective and high-quality agents. Less skilled realtors often choose to go with brokerages that offer them a very advantageous commission split (which I discuss in Chapter 2) or a low flat fee. So, the cycle of mediocrity is perpetuated, with the less qualified realtors making it possible for under-performing brokerage owners to stay in business. This must change.

Third, the bar for entry into the profession is set far too low. It has, in my opinion, always been too easy to enter the real estate profession, and despite governing bodies' efforts to increase professional and educational standards, little has changed. All of us are tarred with the same brush, and those who offer substandard service impact the reputation of the rest. This must also change.

I believe there are three categories of people who aspire to be realtors:

- People who do not know what they want to do in life or don't like their current jobs. These people have not properly researched what is required to become an excellent realtor who earns a good living and provides quality service that he or she can be proud of.

- People who have several family members or friends who either are, or shortly will be, in the market to buy, sell, or lease real estate. They figure they will be able to recoup the costs of becoming a realtor with the first deal or two they close, and make an easy $10,000 plus on subsequent deals, which they are certain they will get based on their friendships and family connections.

- People who see this profession as a serious commitment—one in which they will educate themselves above and beyond the minimum industry standards. They will strive to offer honest, top-notch service to their clients and will thrive because of word-of-mouth referrals.

In order to bring about the required change, there should be more stringent protocols and better training and education to initially qualify as an agent, and recertification courses need to be brought into the twenty-first century. It is beyond belief that realtors in this day and age are not computer savvy, do not know business communication etiquette, have poor (or even disastrous) writing skills, and lack the motivation to upgrade their skills and real estate knowledge. In addition, it should be a bare minimum requirement to be able to conduct business fluently in English or French (depending on one's jurisdiction) in order to negotiate with other agents and understand and explain contracts. This is not to suggest that business ought not to be conducted in other languages; we're a multicultural nation. But contracts are detailed and carry the weight of the law.

Along with the regulatory information that prospective realtors must prove they know, it would make sense to test their ability to speak, read, and write English (or French); soft skills such as effective communication and presentation skills; interpersonal skills; and basic real estate knowledge. If they are deficient in any areas, they should be required to take additional courses to be granted a licence. Another option would be to make the "articling" phase (currently the first two years after a person is allowed to practise real estate transacting in Ontario, during which time that person must complete a few more courses) a true articling period, as it is in the legal profession. Unlike the current articling period (where there is zero oversight required of a new realtor), a brokerage trainer, licensed broker, or brokerage manager should be required to oversee and guide a new realtor's real estate activities and further his or her training and professional development. The broker overseeing the new realtor should receive some continuing education credits for his efforts (and, of course, he would have a competitive advantage to recruit new realtors to his brokerage), but should be held accountable by having to sign off on progress reports. Again, it's difficult to see any drawbacks to employing a similar protocol to that of the legal profession, with its authentic articling requirements, or to that of engineers, who are employed under a P.Eng. while working toward their own P.Eng. designation. What incentive is there for the consumer to hire you to buy or sell a property—especially because you would be representing that consumer in what would likely be one of the largest financial decisions and investments of her life—if you have only a nominal amount of knowledge and basic skills to offer?

Qualities of a Top Realtor

You may aspire to become a skilled and accomplished realtor, but to reach that level you need to run through a character checklist similar to one a start-up business owner would use. Below is a self-assessment checklist, so you can do a self-evaluation; it is also imperative to ask family, friends, and colleagues to fill out an assessment of you as well. It is much better to arrive at the understanding now that realty is not the career for you, than to spend months, or in some cases years, becoming licensed, and investing a substantial amount of money and time learning the business, only to realize down the road what you should have recognized from the beginning.

SELF—ASSESSMENT CHECKLIST

❑ Do you thrive under pressure?

❑ Can you maintain clear thinking and calmness while under pressure?

❑ Are you an outgoing person?

❑ Do you have a positive attitude?

❑ Do you have good interpersonal skills?

❑ Do you like working with or for people?

❑ Are you comfortable engaging people with questions?

❑ Are you a self-motivated person?

❑ Are you a persuasive person?

❑ Are you comfortable negotiating with other people?

❑ Are you good at managing your time?

❑ Are you an organized person?

❑ Are you honest?

❑ Is your relationship with your significant other (wife, husband, or partner) solid?

❑ Are you a good listener?

Are you stable and reliable, especially under pressure? During negotiations, for example, buyers and sellers are often stressed—even overwhelmed—and it is important for their realtor to show calmness, strength, commitment to their wants and needs, and compassion for the difficult aspects of being involved in a real estate transaction.

Are you outgoing and a people person? A successful realtor is always on the go. Just like any other self-employed person, you get out of your career only what you put into it. In order to achieve financial and personal success in this industry, you need to commit to having an ongoing positive attitude and always be thinking one step ahead—whether it is searching for a property, negotiating an offer, or even finding new clients.

I can't emphasize enough the importance of being personable. You are rarely selling a property in this business. Rather, you are constantly selling yourself and the qualities and the services you bring to the table—all without being obvious about it. I often say that if you can get a potential client to like you and feel comfortable with you, you establish a level of trust with that client.

Are you sales oriented and sales motivated? When selling a property, you need to be absolutely committed to the sale. There are open houses to attend, realtors calling you with questions, investigations to be done into the property, meetings with the seller, negotiations that are time sensitive, and so on. If you are someone who enjoys sales, you get through the process much more quickly and with less stress, and you are more likely to maintain a degree of work-life balance. People who are reward motivated tend to thrive in this type of work environment. Remember that there is no base salary flowing into your bank account every two weeks. You receive only what you earn for yourself, and that means you have to sell: sell yourself to prospective clients; continue to sell yourself as the right person for the job once you are working with buyers and sellers; sell a buyer on a property that is right for him, based on his requirements; sell your client's property quickly, for the highest possible price, and on the best possible terms; and sell yourself to your target audience on a daily basis.

For many realtors, work seldom stops. Rarely are they ever *not* busy. Whether you are attending a barbeque, on a cruise, or playing a round of golf, you can expect the topic of real estate to come up, and if it does, you should be ready to sell your knowledge and expertise on the subject—in a discreet way. Just remember that, in the end, selling is espousing someone else's interests or beliefs—with honesty.

Are you good at managing your time? Time management is one of the biggest make-or-break qualities in a realtor. Real estate agents work for themselves, so they rarely have a boss or manager asking if they've completed their to-do list before they leave for the day. This may sound contradictory, since I just said realtors are self-employed, but there are times when they are de facto employees, and even outside of those times, they answer to a broker of record or to an office manager.

Many agents, like myself, work from home. Do you know how easy it is to become distracted in your own home? Canadians watch the most YouTube videos per capita. You might not have gotten around to doing the laundry or grocery shopping the day before. Or, when you're feeling a bit under the weather, it is all too easy to stay in bed for just one day.

Assuming you are able to stay motivated, you still need to strike the right balance between marketing yourself and your listings, doing research for your buyers, scheduling open houses and showings, and being able to juggle hectic negotiations on more than one property at a time, for several different clients, and managing to have a reasonably balanced personal life.

It is also incredibly important today to have a high comfort level with technology. You may not need to know how to build your own website (though doing so would save you some money), but you do need to be comfortable with a computer, using email daily, using a GPS, and using a cell phone (hands-free and Bluetooth earpieces are especially convenient). Here is a roundup of current technology:

- **Contact management or customer relations management (CRM):** Whether you are using Microsoft Outlook or a more sophisticated program such as Salesforce, using a CRM tool effectively can help you plan your time, ensure that you are communicating with prospective clients regularly, keep a centralized ongoing history of activities with a client, and track the value of potential deals that you have in the pipeline. Contact management ties together contact information, communications with customers, and details about clients (birthday, age, marital status, occupation, whether they are condo owners or homeowners, and so on) to help you create lists of contacts based on details gathered. If you have a listing for a starter home, you can create a list of all of your contacts who are married with kids and live in condos, and start calling them to pitch your listing. Having a central repository of historical information and activities can keep your assistant or team in the loop when important calls do come in.

- **Mapping and GPS technology:** Knowing how to use maps and GPS effectively can help ensure that you get from Point A to Point B as quickly as possible. Being late for an appointment can sour a client relationship. If you create online maps that are shareable with potential clients, this can help them find your listings quickly (think "Get Directions" on Google Maps).

- **Websites:** While you needn't have the skills of a web designer, having an attractive and well-laid-out website can invite a prospective client to engage you in using your services as a realtor. Having MLS listings integrated in your website, easy-to-find contact information, and resources to assist in real estate decisions can be reasons for a prospect to keep coming back to your site. Also, understanding concepts in online advertising—search engine optimization (SEO), website analytics, and tie-ins with social media (Facebook, Twitter, LinkedIn, and so on)—can assist you in coming up with an online advertising strategy that tracks the return on your investments and the effectiveness of your online efforts.

- **Online resources and your local library:** If you are a commercial realtor, using demographics from Statistics Canada can help you convince businesses to locate in an area where you have a listing—if those areas hold the target demographics they are looking for. Using the North American Industry Classification System (NAICS) databases at your local library branch for all locally registered businesses can help you create cold-call lists for businesses of a particular industry classification that matches the most closely with your current listing.

- **Modern telephony:** Smartphones such as BlackBerry devices, iPhones, and Android phones allow you to carry your contact information, emails, and social media contacts with you, enabling you to conduct business anywhere. Many voice over Internet Protocol (VoIP) packages with telephone companies allow for features such as "Find Me Follow Me" calling and voice mail as email (useful to archive voice messages).

A very good idea, in addition to taking a character checklist seriously, is speaking with people who have used realtors several times. They can tell you what they liked and did not like about a realtor, and this should provide you with a good sense of whether or not you have what it takes to become a real estate agent (Chapter 20 has many examples of what people like and dislike about realtors).

The most important asset for a great real estate agent is the right attitude, which can be summed up with a few classic words: ambition, initiative, persistence, honesty, and a desire to help.

What Type of Real Estate Is Right for You?

Aspiring realtors have to make a decision as to which type of real estate they will specialize in: commercial or residential. While both have a similar commission structure for sales (4%–5% is the industry standard that the seller pays to the listing brokerage, which the brokerage in turn typically shares with the buyer's agent—confusingly sometimes called the selling agent), residential sales are often less complex and more common than commercial ones. If you have your sights set on a career with a commercial real estate brokerage, you need to make sure that you have financial staying power. For example, when I first started working in the industry with my father, we were gunning for bigger commercial deals and I didn't have a single closing in my first two years with him. However, the first deal I closed was for $8.6 million, which we double-ended (represented both buyer and seller, and so kept the entire commission), at a commission rate of 5%. (This is where I test your quick mental math abilities for the first time—very useful as a realtor, since you are often talking numbers: square feet; frontage; ceiling height; width and depth of a room or lot; commission; interest rate; mortgage payments; net rent; gross rent; taxes, maintenance, and insurance (TMI); and so on.) Residential and commercial types of properties are defined below, followed by a list to explain what is involved for each type.

Residential properties:
- Single-family homes (attached, semi-detached, and detached)
- Residential condominium units
- Cottages and various recreational properties

Residential realtor demands and requirements:
- A flexible schedule: research and work must be done during the day, but evenings and weekends are needed for showings, open houses, listing presentations, and offer negotiations.
- A willingness to learn about a specific product (for example, condos) and specific geographic area.
- A reliable and clean car: there is no better way to spend time with your clients than to drive together to see several properties, rather than following each other or meeting at each property; in addition, sometimes finding parking for two vehicles can be problematic.

Commercial properties:
- Industrial
- Multi-family
- Office
- Retail
- Income-producing
- Land
- Business (qualified commercial realtors can also transact businesses for sale)

Commercial realtor demands and requirements:

- A schedule that is usually tied to business hours (but there are times when you must be available during evenings and weekends).

- A strong understanding of how businesses operate and a willingness to learn a great deal about negotiations and the legal aspect of contracts.

- Staying power: depending on the type of commercial properties you work on, commissions can be fewer and farther between than in residential and, therefore, you need to have sufficient finances to last until your next payday, which may be several months away. (Some new realtors may not complete a deal for an entire 12 months, and even once they do, it can be months between closings. And by "last," I don't just mean living expenses. You have to be prepared to spend money to market yourself and your listings—even more so than residential realtors do.)

Commission Structure

A final note on the difference between residential and commercial work covers commissions. In residential real estate, the total listing commission is typically 5%, with discounts offered by some desperate realtors or in special circumstances, such as if the seller negotiates with you to represent her as a buyer, but only if you sell her house for 4% (while offering 2.5 percent of that to the buyer's realtor). Some communities have gotten into a vicious cycle of commission cutting, where it is now standard practice to take a residential listing for 4%, or even 3%, and often to give part of your commission as a cooperating realtor to your buyer client. The reason I describe the cycle as "vicious" is because only mediocre (or poor) realtors agree to work regularly on a severely discounted commission basis, and once people in the neighbourhood get a taste for discounted commissions, they start to expect it.

Residential commissions are often straightforward, easy to calculate, and paid very promptly to the involved realtors. For the sale of a property, the listing brokerage gets paid something like 3%, 4%, or 5%, and either offers part of that to a cooperating brokerage representing the buyer (sometimes called the selling brokerage, just as the buyer's agent is sometimes called the selling agent) or double-ends the deal if representing both the buyer and seller. If it's on a residential lease, the commission negotiated by the listing brokerage is typically one or two months of rent, or a flat amount; again, part of that amount is offered to the cooperating brokerage. The only real deviation from the above scenario occurs when a listing brokerage gets paid a flat fee to post a listing on the MLS. In that case, a cooperating brokerage normally has to negotiate its commission directly with the seller before presenting an offer. This is a new development, resulting from the Anti-Competition Bureau's 2011 decision to allow outside postings on the MLS in Canada.

Bear in mind that the typical commission received by a brokerage is divided many times, between:

- The listing brokerage and the cooperating brokerage
- Each brokerage and its sales representatives

Also, but less commonly, the commission can be divided between:

- Sales representatives in the same brokerage, who frequently work together
- Members of sales teams

Also, all associated marketing and advertising expenses come out of this commission.

In commercial real estate deals, the commissions can be similar to the set percentage of the sale price common in residential real estate, but they can be more complicated as well. For example, in commercial leasing, commissions can be:

- A certain number of months of the net rent (for example, two months' net rent)
- A certain number of dollars per square foot per year (for example, $1.25 per square foot per year)
- A percentage of the yearly rent, either net or gross (for example, 8% of the first year's net rent, and 4% of the net rent for the balance of the lease term)

Another negotiable element is whether the realtors involved in the initial lease are paid commissions on renewals of that lease (sometimes this is part of the agreement, other times it is not, and sometimes this is agreed to, but only if the same realtors are involved in negotiating or facilitating an eventual lease renewal). It can be more difficult to get paid commercial commissions than residential ones. For example, at the time I am writing this, I have been waiting to be paid for a small commercial lease deal that closed 22 days ago (I represented the tenant). When I spoke with the listing agent last week, he told me he had spoken with the landlord, who said she forgot to pay the commission invoice sent from his brokerage. The listing brokerage had part of the commission in its trust account from the tenant's deposit cheque, but that needed to be topped up by the landlord in order to pay it out to the listing agent and to my cooperating brokerage.

Developing Your Own Style

Whether you're in touch with a potential seller because of a referral, a chance meeting, or diligent marketing and advertising, obtaining the listing depends on how you present yourself—particularly how you establish a rapport and engender trust.

Each realtor develops his or her own style. Sometimes it is an ultra-professional, suit-and-tie style, sometimes it is "your friendly neighbourhood real estate expert," and sometimes it's a laid-back style.

If I had to describe my own style when it comes to interacting with clients and potential clients, I would say that I am casual, open, honest, and knowledgeable. I've never worn a business suit to a real estate meeting. In the summer, I'm more likely to be wearing shorts or capris and a short-sleeved shirt with sandals, rather than jeans or khakis and a dress shirt.

Many of my clients have mentioned that they immediately feel at ease with me because I'm so informal in my interactions with them. I don't believe in meeting someone for the first time and jumping right into his real estate wants or needs. I prefer to get a sense of who the person is and allow him to do the same with me by talking about general topics of interest. For example, when I meet a potential client, we might talk about her neighbourhood, her children, what she does for a living, what she does for fun, or her upcoming vacations or travel plans. This permits each of us to consciously, or more often subconsciously, judge whether the other person is someone we are comfortable with and can trust—or not. We can get a feel for someone we have met in the first five minutes or so, and I've developed this sense by focusing on it consciously. Sometimes after meeting a potential client for the first time, I tell him I feel that a different realtor might be better suited to his needs, because I don't feel comfortable with him, don't trust him, or feel as though our personalities or style of communication would clash down the road.

My clients have learned that I always tell them the truth. Avoid moulding information to suit what a client might want to hear. Although how you present a situation or information to your clients is important, it's more important that you always tell them the truth.

A recent client told me that while she knew homes similar to hers had been selling for $750,000 to $800,000 in her neighbourhood, she wanted to list hers for $850,000. Many realtors would have done so in order to get the listing, but I explained to her that I had to do a more detailed analysis of her home versus the comparables available to us, and advised her that I did not believe listing her property at that price would benefit her.[1] With analysis in hand, I was able to justify my pricing strategy to her, and in the end she said she would depend on my expertise to recommend a listing price to her.

I also believe in letting my clients know when I'm unable to respond to one of their questions, whenever that's indeed the case. There is no reason to be embarrassed when you don't have the answer to a question, and I always tell people I will find out the answer. Realtors who put on airs, or who mislead their clients, potential clients, or other realtors, always have it catch up with them. If you profess to have knowledge of a specific neighbourhood, you could be caught unaware when a local feature becomes an issue in marketing your listing or when dealing with offers. Here are some examples: a cemetery is in the area (even though a recent client of mine finds the quietude a bonus, many people don't), a train passes by several times per night a few streets away from a subject house (which can be heard from the property), or a street is used as a shortcut by hundreds of cars during rush hour (something you wouldn't know unless you know the area well, or are lucky enough to visit the property during those specific times). However, if you admit that you're learning more about the neighbourhood every day, and that you plan on speaking with some of the local experts to get the inside scoop on the area, you cover yourself as well as being very honest and professional.

The Regulatory Bodies

There are three levels of regulation for Canadian realtors:

- **The Canadian Real Estate Association (CREA).** According to its website, CREA:

  - Is one of Canada's largest single-industry trade associations, representing more than 96,000 real estate brokers, agents, and

---

[1] Comparables are properties that have sold and are, preferably, very similar to the subject property in as many aspects as possible, such as geographic location, size, view, neighbourhood influences, amenities, age, type and quality of finishes, quality of construction, and so on. Finding good comparables is one of the most critical steps involved in listing a property; coming up with an offering price for a property; and negotiating a purchase, sale, or lease. Many realtors ignore one cardinal rule: a comparable property must be one that has sold. An asking price merely represents how much a seller would like to obtain (or, sometimes, represents a bluff in a listing agent's sales strategy), but the selling price shows what the market was willing to pay for it. Once a property has sold, it can be used as one of many comparables.

salespeople, and working through more than 100 real estate boards and associations.

- Owns the MLS® and REALTOR® trademarks, which signify a high standard of service and identify members of CREA.

- Operates the www.realtor.ca, www.icx.ca, and www.howrealtors help.ca websites.

- Sets out and administers a code of ethics for registrants in any province who become members. They have an obligation to act in accordance with the REALTOR® code of ethics. This code outlines the accepted standard of conduct for all real estate practitioners who are members of a real estate board or a provincial association.

- **Provincial real estate associations.** For example, the Ontario Real Estate Association (OREA):

  - Is an organization that represents approximately 50,000 real estate salespeople and brokers who are members of Ontario's 42 real estate boards. OREA provides support to, and representation of, its members by producing a variety of written publications and educational programs, and by way of special services. It produces and administers all real estate licensing courses in Ontario.

  - Was founded in 1922 with the mandate to organize licensed real estate activities and provide guidance to the industry throughout the province of Ontario. Some of its goals are to promote high industry standards, protect consumers from unscrupulous salespersons and brokers, and reinforce private property rights.

  - Is committed to educating the public about realtors, enhancing realtors' image, and providing realtors with quality education and professional standards.

  - Produces standard forms for use in the industry, which it updates regularly.

  - Supports educational and charitable cases through its own charitable vehicle, the REALTORS Care Foundation.

- **Local real estate boards.** These organizations:

  - Are typically not-for-profit corporations run by volunteer boards of directors.

- Are geared toward being professional resources for their members, and supporting their members' success.

- Have (mostly) their own codes of ethics, which their members must adhere to.

- Are members of their respective provincial real estate associations (the larger ones), and CREA.

- Design, maintain, and administer multiple listing services (MLS) for their members. This means that each has rules for use of its MLS, and can enforce compliance.

● ● ●

I believe there are three components to qualifying to be a realtor. First, as covered above, you need to have, or be willing to learn and develop, certain attributes and skills. Second, you need to become licensed to practise real estate brokerage in your province. Finally, but perhaps most important, you need to buy into the philosophy that you are your own business. A realtor provides services and therefore you need to continually learn, improve, and upgrade your qualifications. Although this is the second real estate book I have written, and I teach commercial and residential real estate at the university level (University of Toronto School of Continuing Studies for commercial and York University for residential), I am aware that I learn something new with just about every deal I work on. Even though I personally have found formal education to be (mostly) boring, I can't help but take away at least some new knowledge every time I take a course or attend a workshop or webinar. So whether you're licensed or not, improve yourself! There are many real-estate-related courses available. Although they aren't all useful, I challenge you not to learn something new at each one you take.

If you've taken many traditional real estate education courses and no longer feel they can contribute to furthering your education, then I suggest you take a basic accounting course (you're now your own business or you soon will be, so you should have a good grasp of accounting principles), or learn about new technologies that might affect you or your clients (for example, data centre storage, QR codes, search engine optimization, or using photos and videos in your listings), or enrol in a sales program if you feel you could benefit from learning how to be a better salesperson.

In Chapter 2, I discuss how you can find a brokerage that is a good fit.

Finding a Brokerage that Fits

As the focus of this book is on career education, I assume you are licensed to practise real estate. In addition, I assume you've had a criminal record check done and have funds to cover the various membership fees. Now it's time to start shopping for a real estate brokerage, if you haven't already done so. I mention this because you may consider choosing a brokerage before you begin your formal real estate education. A brokerage can offer you guidance and support as you work through the real estate licensing courses, and, even more important in my opinion, you will learn through talking with agents about real-life advice and stories. Tales from the trenches are like classes at the school of hard knocks and invaluable to write down and analyze. Exposure to experience may make a lot of difference for a brand-new realtor who is just starting to look for clients or trying to put his or her first deals together.

Here are the main points to consider when interviewing brokerages and comparing them against each other:

- Commissions and fees structure

- Support and training offered

- Type of brokerage, number of years established, number of agents, and its reputation

These criteria will give you a picture to work with. The main thing to keep in mind is that you want to have the very best in support and training. Can the brokerages you interview provide you with what you need?

Commissions and Fees

These are the criteria that most agents focus on, and with good reason, because any money you pay to, or split with, a brokerage is money that doesn't stay in your pocket. Here is an example of how the commissions are divided up in a typical residential real estate sale, using very basic numbers:

1. Listing brokerage lists the property for sale at $100,000. It receives a 5% commission upon sale.

2. The property sells for $100,000 and the listing brokerage therefore receives $5,000 (plus HST).

3. The buyer is represented by another brokerage, called the cooperating (or selling) brokerage. Because the listing brokerage is offering half of its commission to a cooperating brokerage, it gives 2.5% of the sale price of the property to the cooperating brokerage.

4. The cooperating brokerage therefore receives $2,500 (plus HST) from the listing brokerage.

5. If the buyer's realtor is on a 70/30 (agent/broker) split with his brokerage, he receives $1,750 (plus HST).

Now that we see where the commission comes from and how it is shared in a typical transaction (this can be further complicated in several situations, such as where the buyer's realtor or listing realtor has other realtors or assistants with whom she splits a part of her commission, or where there is a referral fee to be paid by the listing agent or buyer's agent, or where the listing is co-listed between two brokerages), let's look at commission and fee scenarios that many brokerages offer:

- **Split:** This is an arrangement whereby you and your brokerage negotiate a percentage split of any commissions you bring in. I've seen a range of splits from 50/50 (agent/broker) to 65/35, and even to 95/5. The landscape of commission splits has changed over the last decade, from a standard of 50/50 to more creative splits, where the agent can sometimes even choose the services and amount of support he'd like from the brokerage and be charged an appropriate commission split.

- **Fees:** There are several types of fees a brokerage can charge you. The first is a fee instead of a percentage-of-commission split. This is often called a desk fee or a flat fee. It can be $50 per month, or $1,000 per month, or more, and usually depends on the level of services the brokerage is providing to you. Even though $1,000 per month may sound like a lot, consider what a steal that is compared to a 70/30 commission split, if your deals are generating more than $100,000 per year. Flat-fee arrangements can be crafted in a creative way, and if you are persistent, you may get the brokerage to agree to the best possible scenario, which is a percentage-of-commission split until you reach a certain plateau in a calendar year, at which point you don't pay anything more that year, or your plan then switches to a reasonable flat-fee plan.

The other fees to watch for are ones such as telephone system fees and additional desk fees (even if you're on a commission-split plan and you never use a desk at the brokerage office), minimum photo-copying monthly fees, IT or email system monthly fees, brokerage holiday party contributions, brokerage staff appreciation contributions, brokerage charity contributions, no-show fees for brokerage meetings, and so on.

Support and Training

This section is divided into two smaller sections, since one deals with services and products that a brokerage can help you with, and the other deals with training and deal-making support:

- **Services and products:** A brokerage can help you get volume pricing on business cards, real estate signage, marketing and promotional materials, and websites (I would suggest that volume pricing on a website is not as important as your brokerage having good relationships with IDX service and website providers, which I cover in Chapter 7). In-house graphic artists, customizable listing feature sheets, postcards, and just-listed and just-sold flyers are really nice to have. Another important point to consider is whether the brokerage has a lot of walk-ins or call-ins, which can be a great way for you to start your real estate career. Volunteering for the duty desk and being on call to field inquiries at the brokerage level are virtually free ways for you to generate clients.

- **Training and deal-making support:** Depending on your level of experience and comfort in real estate, as well as your general business acumen and skill in negotiations, you should seriously consider trying to find a brokerage that offers strong training programs for its agents. Some top brokerages have ongoing training courses just about every single day. Each course may be offered once or twice a month, so there is almost always a date that you can make for each course, over a period of a few months. Forward-thinking brokerages also hold one-off presentations or courses, often inviting professionals from outside the brokerage to present on topics they are experts in. A brokerage supporting your real estate sales efforts should have experienced senior agents and managers who can walk you through preparing offers, negotiating deals, and helping you out of the problems you and your clients will inevitably be faced with.

Two of the brokerage services you will probably come to appreciate, or lament (if they are not up to par), the most, are the front-desk staff and accounting staff. Having support staff who upload your listings quickly and accurately, and answer client inquiries and forward calls and pages to you promptly, is absolutely invaluable. An accounting department that pays your commissions weekly, via direct deposit, and stays on top of you when condition waivers and other necessary paperwork are due, is such a relief to a busy realtor, because they cover those things so you don't have to worry about them as much.

Type of Brokerage and Community It Serves

The name of the brokerage you are licensed with will be on your business cards, marketing materials, advertising, listings, offers, and so on. Therefore, you should choose a brokerage that represents what you stand for, or, at the very least, is a good fit for you. There are some brokerages that seem to attract realtors of a specific ethnicity, depending on the area. These may not be a good fit for everyone (of that ethnicity, or another one), but if the commission plans and support are appropriate for you, and they are well known and respected in the neighbourhood or type of property you wish to practise in, go for it! These brokerages are particularly suitable if you are of a given ethnic background, speak the language, and understand the culture.

Various brokerages are known to be strong in different markets. For 10 years I worked with a Coldwell Banker brokerage, practising mainly commercial real estate. This was not actually an ideal fit for me, because Coldwell Banker was not known for being strong in commercial real estate (in fact, my understanding is that Coldwell Banker sold its commercial division to Richard Ellis a few decades ago, creating CB Richard Ellis, and only lately has started building its commercial division again. I assume this marks the end of a non-competition clause in the original sale). Despite all this, I had a lot of freedom to practise real estate as I wanted, a respectable commission-split arrangement, and support if I wanted it. However, this was an exceptional situation, and I really suggest you start by determining if you're going to work primarily in residential or commercial real estate, and start looking at a brokerage based on whether they are stronger in residential or commercial.

Make sure that if you plan on running a geo-farming practice (which is where you decide to focus on a certain geographic area and farm it through advertising and marketing) that you're working with a brokerage that is well known and has good penetration in the area you plan on farming. If you think you'll work mainly on downtown condo leasing and sales, it might be a good idea to interview the top three to five downtown condo brokerages. You're going to get services and support tailored to your needs, and maybe even more importantly, you're going to be surrounded by the types of properties you're dealing in, and by realtors who are working in the same markets as you (and remember, as I note in Chapter 5, other realtors are rarely competition, but rather sources of knowledge, expertise, and support).

BROKER INTERVIEW QUESTIONS

General
- What is your company's focus?

- Does your company have a published service commitment?

- What are the major goals for your company and how do you plan to achieve them?

- What market share does your company hold?

- What yardstick do you use to measure your success?

- Do you see yourself as a listing company or one primarily geared toward buyers?

Training
- How do you train new representatives in areas not covered in school (for example, TREB and RECO)?

- What specific training do you have available to make me successful at finding and qualifying buyers?

(continued)

- What training do you have to help me develop my listing skills?

- Who does training in your office and what real estate experience do they have?

- How am I trained, specifically (off the cuff, lecture, role playing, and so on)?

- What other responsibilities does your trainer have?

- Do you have scheduled training programs? If so, what is the schedule?

- Do you have trainers who will go out in the field with me if I need help with my first few transactions?

- May I see your training materials?

- What does training cost me?

Support services

- What software do the secretaries use to assist the sales reps?

- Who is available during the day to answer any questions?

- Who do I see if the broker is busy?

- Is there anyone personally responsible for ensuring that my business is successful?

- How many days a week is the office open and what are the hours?

- How many computers does the company have available to the reps?

- How do you ensure that the support staff are good at their jobs and really care about the business?

- What programs are the support staff trained on?

- Are the support staff trained to greet customers?

- What other services do you offer that will allow me to provide a more complete service to my clients?

- What do the support services cost me?

Technology assistance

- What kind of software programs do you train your reps on?

- Do you provide your software programs at no cost to your reps?

- Is there a contact manager program available at no cost to your reps?

- Which contact manager do you use and/or suggest?

- Do you computer-generate offers? If so, which program do you use?

- Do you have a website? What is the address?

- Who is responsible for the upkeep of your website?

- Are there any costs to the sales reps associated with your website?

- Do I need to purchase my own computer?

- Do you provide any additional training on TREBVision?

- Which programs can I access from my home computer?

- Do you have a computerized listing presentation?

Sales tools and systems

- What marketing tools does the company have for a sales rep to help her do her job more effectively?

- Does the company supply the sales rep with a listing presentation manual (at no cost)?

- Does the company supply the sales rep with a buyer presentation manual (at no cost)?

- Can you show me how you would use the listing presentation manual?

- What tools are available for prospecting? How much do they cost?

- What tools are available to help qualify and control buyers?

- What tools are available to help qualify and service listings?

- What tools are available to help me run a successful open house?

- Does the company have any theme promotions that the sales rep can access?

- What kind of personal promotional materials are available for the sales rep (ad slicks, camera-ready artwork, and so on)?

Business generation

- What does the company do to help the rep generate business aside from giving him a phone and a desk?

(*continued*)

- Do you get any leads or referrals from the broker network?

- Who distributes out-of-town referrals when they come to your office and how are they distributed?

- Do you get any business from your mortgage company? How are these leads distributed?

- How are walk-ins and call-ins distributed?

- Do selling managers or brokers get the walk-in or call-in business?

- How big is your franchise's business referral network?

Office atmosphere

- What does the company do to make the office a fun place to work?

- Does the company have any kind of awards or recognition programs?

- How frequently does the company run contests and what are the prizes?

- Does the company have any kind of annual convention or get-together focusing on business development and networking opportunities?

Commission plans

- Do you maintain a commission plan for your sales reps?

- What kind of commission plan do you have (for example, rent-a-desk, or full-service)

- What kind of franchise fees do I pay? How much per month or year?

- How frequently can I change my plans?

- What can the company do to save costs and pass on the savings to me?

(Source: Coldwell Banker Terrequity Realty Brokerage. Available: www.terrequity.com/brokeragequestions)

How a Brokerage Operates

Since you must be licensed through a brokerage and your deals are processed through that brokerage, you should understand how a brokerage functions and the various skill sets that are necessary to ensuring a smooth operation. One day you might consider owning or running your own brokerage, in which case, this information will be a primer for you.

The following is a list of the personnel a typical real estate brokerage requires in order to operate effectively. In larger or commercial brokerages, there can be additional staff, such as research assistants, marketing managers, and graphic artists.

- **Broker of record:** The licensed real estate broker with whom the regulative responsibilities of the brokerage rest. She may or may not be the owner of the brokerage. If she is not, then normally she is an employee whom the owner pays to use her broker's licence. All brokers of record are real estate brokers, but not all real estate brokers are brokers of record. This is a very important distinction, and it is necessary to understand the distinction to avoid confusion. Many people believe that if you have a broker's licence, you must own or operate your own brokerage. This is not true, and it might be advantageous to obtain your broker's licence as soon as you can, since there is a perception among the public and the profession that having a broker's licence accords you more respect.

  To obtain a broker's licence in Ontario, for example, you must have been registered and working as a real estate sales representative for at least two of the last three years—or have equivalent experience—along with other basic requirements such as being at least 18 years of age, and having paid the appropriate fees. Personally, I let my career get in the way of getting my broker's licence and I waited until 2012 to do so. I regret having waited so long.

- **Broker/owner:** Someone who is both the owner and broker of record for a brokerage.

- **Brokerage owner:** Someone who may or may not be a licensed real estate sales representative or broker, but has chosen *not* to be the broker of record of the brokerage he owns. Instead, he pays a broker to be the broker of record.

- **Manager:** Someone who is typically in charge of one or more brokerage offices. She is the person an agent goes to when he has regulatory issues, questions regarding structuring a deal, questions about what is allowed and not allowed in real estate, and problems with customers and clients.

- **Front-desk staff:** Receptionists, secretaries, data-entry specialists, and administrative employees. They are critical to the operation of a brokerage, because they answer phones, page or email realtors, book and respond to showing requests, upload (called "broker loading") MLS listings to the local real estate board's MLS, receive and file mail and paperwork for realtors, and perform all of the multitude of other tasks, small and large, which pop up on a daily basis in a brokerage. These staff members may not be paid terribly well, so make sure you offer your appreciation for the work they do for you, and encourage your brokerage to retain those employees who are dedicated and industrious. Since these are the people who receive the calls inquiring about real estate assistance, it is important to cultivate a good relationship with them, as they might be able to steer some of those leads your way.

- **Administrative and accounting staff:** A separate department at most brokerages, which takes care of any administrative work that the front-desk staff don't do. The accounting and deal-processing people make sure that the right amounts of money are in the correct brokerage bank accounts (operating account, trust account, and commission trust account); receive, track, refund, and deposit funds into the appropriate account; deposit cheques for deals; remind realtors when conditions are due, or deadlines are approaching; issue invoices for commissions payable by lawyers or other brokerages; process payroll for brokerage staff, as well as for realtors (which, of course, includes your commissions); track any applicable company or brokerage awards, run contests, prepare and send out brokerage newsletters, and much more.

- **Human resources and licensing staff:** Some brokerages, often the larger ones, assist managers or the broker of record by hiring staff who in turn stay on top of hiring (and terminating) staff for the brokerage, licensing and certification, and real estate regulations work. These staff ensure that all real estate regulations are followed by the brokerage (such as the length of time records are kept by the brokerage), and ensure that all real estate salespersons at the brokerage are up to date with their continuing education requirements, and are in good standing with the provincial regulatory body and local real estate boards.

- **Realtors:** Without realtors, brokerages would have a hard time staying in business! These can be part- or full-time sales representatives or brokers.

How a Brokerage Makes Money

Exactly what business is a real estate brokerage in? Well, like most other for-profit businesses, it is in the business of making money for its owners.

Brokerages usually earn revenues by charging a commission percentage on deals made by the brokerage's realtors, or by collecting various fees from them. However, to illustrate that all is not flowers and honey for owners of brokerages, the Real Estate Council of Ontario (RECO) reported in 2010 that only 7 out of 10 brokers of record were active in listing or selling real estate, while others were involved in generating other sorts of revenue (which generally means they were not full-time brokers of record and had other businesses). Just as is the case in any business, owning a real estate brokerage is not a guarantee of making huge profits.

What this means for you is that you should try to be involved with a brokerage that has the same values as you do. Hopefully, you want to be a successful realtor, so find a successful brokerage. As with most things in life, the cheapest solution is rarely the best solution. Find a brokerage that offers a balance of value for cost.

Be sure to meet with the owner (and the broker of record, if they are not the same individual), and ask her what her vision is. Ask what type of realtor she is looking to add to her company and how she sees you fitting in. Ask her what she believes the formula for success is for a realtor, and whether she feels you could find that with her.

Online Brokerages

I'm only going to mention one online brokerage website, TheRedPin (www.theredpin.com), which is one of a new variety of online brokerages.[1] Many of these sites have bigger databases than MLS, achieved by aggregating public MLS data and data from other property websites to provide online viewers with thousands of up-to-date listings. They often offer some brokerage services at below-market pricing, which they are able to do based on:

- Users doing a lot of the leg work and searching for properties themselves (which, in my opinion, is akin to telling a 16-year-old to go and research and find his own car to buy, as he knows what a car

---

[1] For additional reading on TheRedPin, see the article available at: www.thestar.com/ business/article/1136370—toronto-real-estate-traditional-realtors-face-challenge-by-online-players.

is, what many of the features are, which colour he likes, and how much different models cost—but does he have the life experience and wherewithal to compare gas mileage, financing versus leasing, maintenance costs, reliability of each model, and so on?).

- The use of their digital platform to gain and manage customers, which provides a number of business efficiencies.

In the future, online brokerages will have the ability to grab and aggregate more public real estate listings as part of their service, and Internet-savvy consumers can get a good idea of what the current market is offering in terms of pricing and property information, although they may not be able to properly analyze and interpret that information. Something to keep in mind is that 95 percent of buyers are now starting their search online, but most of them use a professional to broker any deal they make.

Internet data that is freely available and easily collected is allowing for sites like TheRedPin to create valuable data-driven perspectives on properties that have never been available before.

● ● ●

Now that you understand how a brokerage operates and why selecting the right one is essential to your success as a realtor, Chapter 3 breaks down the money side of real estate and how you find clients.

How Do You Make Money and Find Clients?

The Money Part

It's critically important to keep this in mind and repeat it to yourself every day: Being a realtor means running your own business. Therefore, you have your revenue (hopefully), your expenses (there are always more than you expect or would like), and then your profits (or losses). Obviously, your goals are to maximize your revenue, minimize your expenses, and have a healthy profit every year. Just because you are profitable, however, does not mean that you have a regular income. Because closings can be spread apart, you should budget and plan for dry spells, so that you can weather them financially.

Most people know that real estate agents typically work on a commission basis. This means that we get paid a portion of the sale or lease price of a property, normally paid when the transaction closes. However, this is not always the case. I have a client that took one year to pay my commission, in monthly instalments, for a 10-year lease I arranged for his retail space with a triple-A tenant. I didn't like this arrangement, but it wasn't worth souring our relationship (we had done other deals and I expected to do more). I do, however, wonder if he would have made his lawyer, accountant, or architect wait a year before settling their bill. Even when you are paid promptly, which is usually the case, you split part of the commission with your brokerage. Let me put this into numbers:

- **Best-case scenario:** If you receive a $10,000 commission and you pay only $500 to your brokerage, you still have to pay your expenses and your income taxes. You're left with approximately $7,000 (and that puts you into a very low tax bracket).

- **Worst-case scenario:** If you get a $10,000 commission and you pay half of it to your brokerage (don't assume this is crazy, since, as I explain in Chapter 2, many realtors accept paying a large percentage to their brokerage if the support services are stellar, the brand recognition is high, and there are regular leads provided by the brokerage), you still have to pay your expenses and then your income taxes. You could be left with as little as $1,500–$2,000.

Many realtors who have the basic required skills, along with true drive and determination, can make a successful living in this game. Earning six figures is not out of reach (in fact, at my brokerage, every year the same handful of agents each have gross commission income close to the $1-million mark). However, if you're not meant for this job (if you don't have the drive, sales persona, acute business and interpersonal skills, and so on), then you're better off realizing that early on, because many realtors don't make enough money to survive with real estate sales as their full-time job (and as discussed elsewhere, full time is really the only way to do it well). Some people practise real estate brokerage as a hobby, a second job, or a part-time job. In Toronto, various studies over the years have shown that approximately 20 percent of the agents at the Toronto Real Estate Board (TREB) do approximately 80 percent of the real estate transactions every year. I'm sure this is not far from the truth at most real estate boards in Canada.

I'm not afraid to remind my clients or potential clients that I work on a contingency basis, and that what seems like a lot of money in their eyes, which I get paid at the end of a successful transaction, takes into account the two, five, ten, or more deals that I need to work on to have just one that works out. I should mention, though, that as a realtor's skills and his or her ability to choose the clients he or she works with increase, more and more of the deals he or she works on culminate in a closing.

Remember that as a real estate agent, you are your own business and therefore you need to obtain an HST or business tax number from the Canada Revenue Agency. Your brokerage pays you HST on your commissions, which you need to remit to the government. Since a business is allowed to deduct some expenses from its revenues for tax purposes, and doing so lowers the amount of taxes it needs to pay, it is important that you find a qualified bookkeeper, at minimum, and potentially also an accountant, to guide you in your taxation strategy.

Most brokerages provide you with comprehensive deal summaries, a clear calculation of the total commission on each deal, the split between the two brokerages, the split between the brokerage and you, the HST amount, and any expenses it has deducted. If you keep a detailed record of your business-related expenses (which includes keeping your receipts somewhat organized), then it should be a relatively simple job for a bookkeeper or accountant to prepare your tax returns.

Any shortcomings in provincial real estate education in Canada are related mainly to deal-making, business, interpersonal skills, and general industry knowledge. Most of the provincial real estate associations seem to do quite a good job at guiding and educating members and students about liability and how to avoid getting into sticky situations, from a legal perspective. Realtors can be sued by consumers. Most complaints from consumers can be handled, in order of escalation: by a realtor, by a realtor's brokerage, through the local realtor's real estate board, and, finally, at the realtor's provincial real estate association level. The worst-case scenario is to be sued by a consumer, in which case your errors and omissions (E&O) insurance comes in handy (insurance coverage is typically arranged by your provincial real estate association and is a condition of your membership). Be sure to read about which specific instances of liability are covered by your E&O insurance, and which are not. For example, in Ontario, the E&O insurance arranged by the Real Estate Council of Ontario covers acts of negligence by its members, but not fraudulent or dishonest acts. Most E&O insurance policies call for an increase in the insured registrant's deductible with every claim.

The Clients Part

Where do clients come from? How can I find them? Or, how can they find me? The answer is that your clients can come from anywhere and everywhere. The challenge for agents is twofold:

- Finding leads (potential clients)
- Having potential clients feel and think that you are the right person to assist them with their real estate needs

Much of this book is meant to address the second point, but the rest of this chapter is given to the question of finding clients. When I was younger, my father often quoted a proverb to me that I share with you here: you can lead a horse to water, but you can't make it drink. Indeed, everything in this chapter can help you in finding clients, but you still need to do the hard work yourself.

Here are some of the more traditional ways of finding new clients (which still work, if you are willing to put in the effort):

- **Get out there and look:** Fellow realtors have told me stories of client relationships beginning in a line-up at Tim Hortons, at a child's hockey or soccer game, at a religious gathering, at a wedding, at a funeral, in a car accident (although I don't suggest you set this up, but if you do get into a minor car accident, make sure you give the other person your card!), at the gym, at the dentist's or doctor's office, and from other service providers such as insurance salespeople, bank tellers, dog walkers, and so on.

- **Door knocking:** This strategy sounds like a nightmare to most people because it takes guts and a thick skin, but you might be surprised at the contacts you can make by getting to know people by going door to door in a given neighbourhood.

- **Cold calling:** Calling strangers is similar to door knocking, but you don't have to physically be there. You do need to ensure that you are not violating Do Not Call List legislation.

- **FSBOs:** You can approach these people at their properties, but keep in mind that you're one of many doing so; therefore, make sure you're polite, professional, and helpful. You can also call FSBOs. I know some realtors who go on FSBO (For Sale By Owner) websites and call many sellers, asking if they can be of any assistance, or asking to set up showings. If you make the right impression and the FSBO has a hard time selling his property, you could be asked to list his property for sale.

- **Open houses:** As I discuss in Chapter 8, hosting open houses can be a good way to meet people who are not represented by a realtor.

- **Expired listings:** This one is tricky, but if you can find listings in which the seller does not specifically indicate that you cannot contact her upon expiry of the previous listing, then it's a great lead, because the person obviously wanted to sell if she had listed her property. You are going to have to present a compelling case, however, as to why you'll be successful where the previous agent was not.

- **Referrals:** It is always easier to do a good job and have people praise you to others than to spend time and money looking for new clients.

Some more modern or progressive ways of finding clients are the following:

- **Make friends at your brokerage:** Your manager and the front-desk staff are the first ones to know when a lead comes in, and if they feel confident handing leads off to you, you should get some calls.

- **Your website:** If you have a professional site that ranks well in search engines, you can get quality leads from it.

- **Online advertising:** Sites such as Google, Facebook, Yahoo!, and so on enable you to pay for ad impressions or clicks through to your website. This can work, but can become very expensive if you don't understand how they work and you're in a highly competitive real estate brokerage area such as Toronto.

- **Real estate signs, posters, and billboards:** Although these have all existed for a long time, there are new ways to interact with potential clients, like having them text or scan QR codes to receive more information on a property, or to register their information with you to be sent properties or real estate information.

- **Become valuable to a builder:** If you are successful in selling a large number of a builder's or developer's properties, you can ask them to give you priority access to future developments and properties.

Of course, when deciding which of the strategies above to use, it's always going to be a question of time or money—either you have the time or you have the money. If you're starting out, you don't have any clients and therefore have a small marketing budget. You need to understand that you'll have to work day and night to scrounge up leads. However, if you have a healthy budget and you're already moderately busy working on real estate deals, you can't dedicate much time to lead generation, so you'll likely spend more money to make sure you keep your lead pipeline full.

Creating Relationships and Making Connections

The list below is only one guide for creating relationships and making profitable connections, as there are many theories and approaches for new realtors getting started.

Kick-start your prospecting:

- Think of, and write down, every name in your circle of influence. Call and let them know what you do.

- Visit open houses.

- Host open houses for other realtors.

- Learn how to approach FSBOs.

- Explore expired listings to see if you can find any you are allowed to approach (due to privacy legislation).

- Spend time at your brokerage's opportunity/duty desk (this is now often done not physically at the brokerage, but simply by making yourself available, during a specific period of time, to have inquiries forwarded to your phone from the brokerage).

Form a real estate database of potential buyers and sellers from:

- Your circle of influence

- Referrals requested from your circle of influence

- Names obtained while on opportunity/duty time

Specialize and prepare an appropriate marketing plan:

- Geographically: create a "geo-farm" area you will work within and become an expert on

- By property type: residential or commercial is the first decision, but there are many subcategories:

  - Rentals

  - Sales

  - Single-family homes

  - Residential condos

  - Offices

  - Industrial

  - Medical buildings

- Multi-family homes

- Land

- Income-producing properties

Get to work (intelligently) by:

- Setting realistic benchmarks and goals for prospecting, door knocking, cold calling, listing presentations, and so on.

- Cutting up your week into half-hour slices, and deciding when you'll do the above.

- Tracking how much each lead and finished deal costs you, in both time and money, once you start doing some deals. This allows you to determine where best to spend your marketing and advertising dollars, and where to spend your time (you learn quickly that you only have so much of it!).

● ● ●

I finish this chapter with a brief story that I hope inspires you to be creative when thinking of how and where to find leads and clients. A realtor at my brokerage has only been licensed for a couple of years, but he's done 25-plus transactions each year. His secret? He lives in a downtown Toronto condo building and regularly walks his dogs. Yup, that's it. He realized early on that he was approachable when walking his two dogs, and that the downtown dog community is quite sociable. He shapes his lead generation around this, and even made his dogs part of his image by having the picture of himself on his business cards include his dogs. He meets many people when walking his dogs and carries his business cards with him all the time. After the first year of doing a lot of condo leasing, he started getting repeat business and a cycle of referrals. Now he's closing many condo and house sales and hasn't looked back.

Now that you know how and where to source clients, you need to know how to serve them professionally, honestly, and profitably. Part II covers representing the seller and what you need to consider when you meet a client who is considering selling his property.

PART

II

Representing the Seller

When Meeting with a Client

Putting a Client at Ease

Now that you've had a chance to think about how you want to appear to potential clients, you should consider the clients' situations when suggesting where to meet with them the first time. Usually, when you are first meeting a potential seller, it makes sense to meet at his or her home whenever possible. This allows you to see the property you may be representing, and the seller is most likely to feel "at home" when discussing his or her motivation for listing the property for sale. There are, however, exceptions to this. Don't be insistent or offended if a seller prefers to meet elsewhere. Perhaps his home is messy or dirty, and he wants to tidy and clean up before you see it. He may have a complicated personal situation at home and feel that having someone over would be easier in a week or two. Or you may be dealing with a seller who lives alone and feels it prudent to meet a stranger for the first time in a public place, where the seller can determine whether or not to invite the realtor into her home at a later date. In these instances, suggest meeting somewhere that will complement your business style, such as a public library, a coffee shop, your brokerage's office, and so on. If the first meeting goes well, it's logical for you to suggest that your next meeting take place at the seller's house so that you can see it before listing it.

If you meet your potential seller at his home, be on time and don't forget your manners. A pleasant attitude and ready smile go a long way toward starting off on the right foot. It's better to cancel a first meeting than to go in a bad mood or with a negative attitude.

You should also bring the following, depending on your style:

- A notepad or laptop to facilitate note-taking.

- Your business cards and a portfolio of marketing materials.

- A listing presentation (more on this below).

- A camera. (Although I don't suggest you take pictures of the listing at your first meeting, it can be useful to have a camera. For example, I recently told a seller I would find out if a window manufacturer still made a small lever that was missing on her window, by taking a picture of the window and the lever on another window in her house.)

When I go to a first meeting with a seller, my preference is to sit down where she is most comfortable in the house and get to know each other. The seller often asks whether you want to sit down and talk or take a tour of the house first, so I suggest you reply with something like, "Why don't we sit down and chat for a bit, then you can show me around your home?" By initially sitting down and talking, you're able to get a sense of the seller's personality, her likes and dislikes, and, if you ask the right questions, you should have a good feel for the house before you tour it. For example, before the tour, you should know:

- Whether there are any serious issues with the house that may require repairing or addressing

- Whether the seller is open to staging (is staging necessary, or even a good idea, based on the type of property, the neighbourhood, and what the market is like at that time?)

- Who lives in the house

- How flexible the seller is going to be about showings

- If there are fixtures or chattels you need to be aware of, which the seller really wants to leave or take with her

When you tour the house with the seller, make sure that you are honest but polite and understanding. Many homes you see are not perfectly neat, and many sellers are self-conscious about this. If you truly like a painting or artwork, a specific piece of furniture, or a child's drawing, say so. Various features of the house are also appropriate things to comment on, such as unusual or beautiful wood or tile flooring, a nice bathroom, or the view from a window or backyard. Continue to ask the potential seller questions while on the tour. This allows you to continue to gather information, making you more informed and professional down the road, and it also keeps the seller talking, which is one of the most important things a salesperson can do— talk less than a client or potential client. People generally like to talk about themselves, and they especially like to talk about their homes when they have an appreciative and attentive audience. It is important that you point out relevant things, if you feel the seller is open to hearing them, for example, certain furniture that would be ideal for staging, and features you would highlight in the listing and marketing materials. However, only make these comments if you are sure of what you are saying. If you're not a hardwood floor expert, don't pretend you know the type of flooring they have. Ask first, then build on the seller's response if it is within your knowledge bank.

Your first meeting should conclude with pleasantries, just as it should have started, and a commitment on the next steps. If you agreed that you would be listing the house, great. Tell the seller you'll see him soon—to sign the listing documents (if you haven't brought the listing documents with you, in which case you want to get them signed as quickly as possible— preferably, later that same day or the next day), to take pictures, and to get some more information from him. If the seller said he would like to see some area comparables to get a sense of the potential pricing, then tell him how and when you'll get those to him, or set up a meeting so you can go over them together.

I should tell you that I rarely do a listing presentation (marketing materials you prepare for the listing, open houses, advertising, online presence, and industry and buyer contacts). I'm not a big believer in them. Once a seller feels comfortable with me and trusts me, she most often lists her property with me. I feel as though formal listing presentations make the atmosphere too serious, and, frankly, all realtors have access to, or can access, the same selling features of a listing presentation.

While many realtors go to listing presentations with the listing documents typed up and ready for signatures, this doesn't jive with my low-pressure, "take your time to feel comfortable" style. Even if potential clients want to work with me when I first meet them, they should still want to work with me later on or the next day, when I typically send or deliver the listing documents for signing. If they don't, I really don't want to work with them.

My daughter just finished her first year of school, and her teacher apparently did not know what I did for a living. Since I had helped her source some materials during the school year, she knew that I was resourceful, and asked me in an email if I knew a good realtor who could help her sell her home. I was happy to respond and proceeded to give her a summary of my qualifications.

We bumped into each other a few days later in a local restaurant, and she said she had just been talking about me with her friend, and she wanted me to list her property for sale. We set a day and time to meet, agreeing it would make sense to meet at her house so I could have a look at it.

I arrived at her home a few minutes early and we sat down in her living room. She explained to me that she had decided to move from Toronto to Montreal and what her timing was to sell in Toronto and to buy in Montreal, and her financial considerations and goals. We talked a little bit about pricing in her neighbourhood, but I told her I couldn't suggest an asking price, having just seen her house for the first time. I let her know that I would prefer to do a tour of the house, and when back in my office, do detailed comparison research. I explained to her how being represented by a realtor works, who pays whom, and the various representation scenarios that can develop. She was somewhat familiar with multiple representation, as she had walked into an open house without representation and the listing agent had double-ended the deal when she purchased the house.

Double-ending takes place when the listing agent has a buyer who is not represented by a realtor purchase the property. Many realtors try to set up this situation, because they usually make double the commission. I try not to sweat it, and focus on selling the property as quickly as possible, for the most money possible, on the best terms possible for my client. Then I'm on to the next deal. I have experienced several deals where the listing agent sabotaged offers from buyers' agents, just so he could give himself space to find his own buyer, and, in the end, he didn't find any buyers. In that case, the seller and the listing agent both lose.

Because her house was in a desirable area of downtown Toronto, I knew it would sell quickly if priced right. She agreed to have a home inspection done so that we could provide it to potential buyers. However, she had already identified a few issues in the house, so I suggested we have a pre-inspection done, which would give us detailed information on any further problems in the house (which most buyers would discover when doing their own inspection) that we could rectify, and then have the final home inspection done. This strategy would result in a much cleaner home inspection report. We walked around the house and I pointed out a few things she should take care of before I listed the property, and we talked about preparing the property by doing a deep cleaning and de-cluttering, and some minor staging. She then got all the documents she had relating to the property, which I took to scan and keep on file in case I needed to refer to anything down the road. These included the agreement of purchase and sale for her current house; the home inspection report; maintenance and repair invoices; and receipts and warranties for major purchases (appliances, wooden floors, new garage door and door opener, and so on).

Then something happened that is quite rare in our industry, and really demonstrates how important it is to choose the clients you will work with. Just before I left, she said that she wanted to know how we could market the property to maximize my chances of double-ending the deal so that I would keep the entire commission. It was one of the most selfless, considerate, and thoughtful things a client has ever said to me. I told her how much I appreciated her thoughtfulness, and that if a multiple representation situation presented itself, I would be comfortable handling it (although I reminded her that she and the buyer would need to both be comfortable with it as well), but my goal in representing a seller is always to sell for the highest price on the best possible terms. I added that I would rather do 30 deals in a year where I represent one side, than try to constantly double-end deals and only do 10 in one year.

At the end of the day, there were three potential buyers who did not have their own realtor (all of whom were amenable to allowing me to represent them), but her house sold to a young couple who did have a realtor. Although some realtors might have been a little disappointed at this outcome, I was happy: the house sold for a price, and on terms, that my client was comfortable with, and the listing did not drag on forever, allowing me to move on to the next deal.

Helping a Client with the Fine Print

This next story is a hypothetical situation involving a friend I refer to here as Scott, and a lesson he learned. It illustrates why I feel it is important to be as giving as possible with one's professional time when it makes sense to do so (and when a friendship is involved, I always try to give as much of my time as I can afford to).

My friend Scott asked me to help him find a house to buy more than five years ago. He ended up buying a semi-detached townhouse in Pickering, Ontario, just off Highway 401. Eighteen months ago he asked me if I could send him a few properties for sale in Pickering larger than his current one.

I sent Scott a few listings that were on the market, and set him up to automatically receive new listings via email. When we talked a little later, he mentioned that he was not in a rush to buy because he wanted to wait until his wife was working full time, which would allow them to more easily qualify for a new (and likely larger) mortgage. I emailed him every four to six months, asking if there was anything I could do, or if there were any properties that had caught his eye. Scott was never quite ready to move ahead, but was always appreciative of my offers of assistance.

My sister happened to live in the same townhouse complex as Scott, and asked me one day if I knew that Scott was selling his house. I sent him a quick email congratulating him on listing his home, letting him know that I would still be happy to help him with anything he needed, and suggesting that he may want to send me any offers he received or presented, because it was often good to get another perspective. Also, I might have had some strategic suggestions that his realtor might not have thought of. Scott did call me and we had a good talk. He explained that the realtor they had listed with was a friend of his wife's father, and that they were only paying him a 1% commission (but still wisely offering the cooperating brokerage 2.5%, to ensure they received reasonable interest from realtors who had buyer clients), because he and his wife were creating a website featuring their property, and they would be preparing and paying for all the staging and property preparation. Scott added that in exchange for listing the property at a low commission rate, they would be using the same realtor to buy their next home. I reiterated that I would be very happy to help in any way I could, and looked forward to hearing how things went.

Scott sent me an email a few days later to let me know their townhouse had sold after being on the market for only one day. I told him I was very glad that the sale had gone well for them.

A few weeks later, Scott emailed me asking if I could send him comparables for a property they were thinking of buying. I put a few together and fired them off. He called me not too long afterwards and told me about a suitable property they had found without their realtor. They felt that they were getting it for a good price, and it had a basement apartment with a long-term tenant who would be staying. I wished him luck.

A few months went by and Scott called me out of the blue. He said he needed some advice. He sounded a little perturbed, and, because he was a level-headed and steady person, I was curious about what was going on. He explained that the closings for both his townhouse sale and the purchase of his new home were coming up in a couple of weeks. He had received an invoice from the listing brokerage for 5% of the sale price, but because he and the brokerage had agreed on a total commission of 3.5%, he was confused and concerned. He had not contacted his realtor yet, because he wanted to know where he stood before speaking with his realtor or the brokerage. I asked him a lot of questions, including whether he had signed a listing agreement with his realtor. He had, so I walked him through it, looking for the paragraph on the 3.5% commission, and also the section where it laid out that 2.5% would be paid to the cooperating brokerage. Once he confirmed these two points, I suggested that he contact the listing brokerage or his realtor to let them know they had made a mistake. Because so many residential listings are at 5%, I thought an honest mistake had been made—one that Scott had caught in time.

Just as I was about to end the call, I had a thought. I asked Scott if he remembered signing a buyer representation agreement (BRA). Yes, he told me, that was the form he had just been looking at. No, I told him, that was the listing agreement to sell his house; a BRA was used to lay out the terms of a relationship with a brokerage, which assisted in finding and negotiating the purchase of a property. Scott remembered signing a document like that, and said he would look for it. I asked him to email it to me when he found it. Instead, five minutes later, he called to say that he had found the BRA. I asked him to look for a section that talked about the commission. He said it had "2.5%" written down. I had him check that he and the brokerage had both signed the BRA, and that he had purchased his new home while the BRA was in effect, and he confirmed that was the case.

Then I told him I had some bad news for him—he owed the brokerage 2.5% of the purchase price. Scott said he was already paying 3.5%, so I explained that there were two separate deals: the sale of his house, for which he was paying the listing brokerage 3.5%, and the purchase of his home, for which he owed the brokerage 2.5%. Furthermore, I explained that a BRA was typically used so that a buyer knew he would be getting good service from a realtor, because he was committing to that realtor; and because the realtor knew she would be paid if her client bought something, she would likely work diligently at it. Because Scott's realtor had not explained this well, I gave Scott a five-minute primer on the BRA: It is a document in which a buyer agrees to use a brokerage to search for and negotiate the purchase of a property of a certain type (this can be more or less precise—for example, commercial versus office, or residential versus a semi-detached house), in a given geographic area (for example, an imaginary quadrant bordered by North Street, South Road, East Avenue, and West Drive), and during a set period of time. The duration of the BRA is negotiable.

If a buyer is loathe to sign one, but a realtor says he has the perfect property and he'd like a one-day BRA so that he is protected (protected in that he will be paid a commission for sure), then even the most reluctant BRA-signer may agree. I typically ask for a six-month BRA, but I can often settle on three or four months. Many buyers don't understand why the duration of a BRA should be so long. However, I explain to them that there is a learning curve to working together, and even for them to discover, with my guidance, what they really need and want in a property. Many buyers who think they know what they need and want are sorely mistaken, and often end up buying something different from what they had originally imagined (for example, if a buyer absolutely needs three washrooms, she will often settle for two, or if a buyer thinks that the garage has to fit two cars, she may end up buying a property without a garage).

A BRA also states that the buyer is agreeing to forward all properties he comes across to his realtor. Further, it is stated clearly that the cooperating brokerage, the buyer's brokerage, will always try to obtain a commission from the listing brokerage or seller, and that in the event that it is not able to do so, it will inform the buyer that should he elect to present an offer on that specific property, he will be paying his brokerage's commission. I always tell my buyer clients that before I even send them a property to review, I'll let them know whether the seller or listing brokerage won't pay my commission. If that is the case, I tell them that they should budget for my commission when coming up with the maximum price they are willing to pay for the property in question. In Canada, though, this may sound unusual, since 95 percent of the time or more the seller pays the listing brokerage, which in turn pays the cooperating brokerage. When presented and practised properly, getting a BRA signed by your clients should not be a huge issue. If your clients have been educated to understand that they are receiving true value from you, they will also understand that, for the right property, it is worth paying your commission.

I had a client who was looking for an income-producing property that he could relocate his successful IT company to, while keeping several tenants to help pay for the property. We came across a really good candidate after looking for several months. The asking price was $1.7 million, and it was worth every penny. However, the MLS listing showed that the listing brokerage was offering only a $10,000 commission to the cooperating brokerage. I called the listing agent, who explained that he did a lot of work with this client, and because his client was the third mortgagee (the third lender in line, registered on title of the property), and was potentially going to lose some money, the brokerage was not willing to pay very much in commission. I spoke with my client and explained the situation to him. He agreed to sign a BRA for this property, whereby he would pay us an additional $30,000 commission. When we prepared an offer, I told the listing agent that we were coming in at full asking price, even though our offer was only for $1.67 million, since my client had to budget to pay the majority of my commission.

Once I had explained all of this to Scott, I could tell from the tone of his voice that he was quite worried. With only two weeks to go until his sale and purchase closing, and having budgeted everything carefully, he must have been wondering where he was going to come up with more than $10,000 to pay this unplanned commission. I suggested that he wait and see what the brokerage said or sent to him. Scott had proof that the brokerage had agreed to list the property for 3.5%, and he might only need to address the additional 2.5% for his new house if the brokerage brought it up.

We spoke a few more times in the following days. Often, Scott wanted just to update me and ask a few questions, but one day he called me on speakerphone with his business partner, in the middle of what appeared to be a strategy brainstorming session about the commission issue. I participated for about 20 minutes, and reiterated that Scott should argue the 5% since he was in the right on that, and wait for any notice from the brokerage regarding the 2.5%, if it ever came. He said that he had found a letter from his realtor saying that he wished Scott and his wife luck with their house search, because he did not feel they could find one in the area they wanted, at the price they were willing to pay. The letter was quite clearly a "thank you for your business, and best of luck" letter. I warned him that he should work quickly to resolve things with the brokerage because he didn't want the closing day to come and for him to find out that the brokerage had registered a lien against one, or both, houses, which would prevent the closings from occurring.

A week later, Scott left me a voice mail message thanking me for being such a good friend, and letting me know how much he appreciated my professionalism and generosity with my time.

A few weeks later he called me to say that both deals closed smoothly. He had spoken with the listing brokerage's broker of record, gotten along very well with her, and she had cleared everything up and he did not have to pay anything extra.

If I had to put a moral to this story, there would likely be several:

- **Realtors:** Spend as much time as necessary to properly explain documents to your clients. You can be a superstar realtor whom your clients love for six months, but if they feel you did not explain something important, or if they were side-swiped by a problem or issue that you could have prepared them for, you will become the devil in their eyes. This is very important to remember if you consider that many successful realtors get 90 percent of their business or more from referrals.

- **Buyers and sellers:** Only sign documents you fully understand. You cannot make a real estate transaction without signing contracts at some point, but you must ask for clarification for as long as it takes for you to understand.

- **Friends (realtors, buyers, or sellers):** Many people believe they should not mix friendships and business. While I know things sometimes go wrong, I truly believe a friendship is a great reason for doing business together. First, you already trust each other, which I think is the greatest obstacle to successfully completing a deal. Second, you simply have to have the mindset that you won't allow to affect your friendship. I have represented many friends in real estate, and there have been times when we've argued. During those times, I did everything possible to ensure that our friendship was not affected—I once even gave up my commission when there was a misunderstanding about a financial factor of the deal.

Although I did spend a few hours helping out my friend with headaches that he could have avoided if he had used me as his realtor, I'm confident that Scott will now refer me to his friends and associates when the opportunity presents itself, not only because he knows now that I am good at what I do based on the suggestions I gave him, but also from a sense of obligation, due to the amount of time I gave to him providing advice, even when I really didn't have to do so.

● ● ●

You've met with your seller client and she would like you to list her property. How do you agree on a price at which to list the property? I cover this seemingly simple but often complicated art form in Chapter 5. Also, when offers come in, you need to know how to coach her through working with an offer, even if it is not what the client was hoping to receive, so that you can move toward an acceptable conclusion.

Pricing Strategies

Factors to Consider in Establishing an Asking Price

Recently, a repeat client called me who had two investment condo units in Toronto and a six-year tenant in one condo who had just given her notice that he'd be leaving in just over two months. Being conservative, she wanted to ensure that her unit would not be vacant for any period of time. She therefore asked me to list the unit for lease immediately. I explained that I would look at the recently leased comparables in her condo building and in the area. My client's current tenant was paying $1,550 per month, and my client wanted to increase the rent, as that amount had been set several years ago. I was pleasantly surprised when the MLS did not have any other units for lease in her building, and I suggested a listing price of $1,995. I arrived at that price by taking the following factors into consideration:

- Currently, Toronto is in a landlord's market, and bidding wars for rental condo units have not been unusual over the past year.

- Any rental units in the same building had been leased in less than 10 days during the last year.

- All rentals in my client's building had been leased for the asking price over the last year.

- There was little supply of similar condo units in a 500-metre radius around the subject condo building.

- Although I would have liked to get over $2,000 per month in rent for this unit, I knew how realtors and consumers search the MLS, and potential tenants would have been lost if we asked for more than $2,000.

In the end, the unit was leased in just under two weeks, for full asking price, with both the first and last months' rent as a deposit, plus a second deposit equivalent to four months of rent as security with the tenant's father's guarantee of the lease (in Ontario, a landlord cannot demand more than first and last months' rent, so in some cases, when both parties are in agreement, creative arrangements are arrived at to secure a lease).

Different situations call for diverse pricing strategies. Here are some of the main scenarios, assuming a market that is relatively stable—neither super hot, nor horribly slow:

- Attractive property in good condition, possibly with substantial upgrades and renovations, which will garner much attention and likely several offers. You have three approaches you can take with pricing here, each with its own set of pros and cons:

  - List below market:

    - Pro: You may be able to get a bidding war going, which can result in offers that are higher than what the market would otherwise dictate.

    - Con: It may be too obvious to buyers and their realtors, and if they are like me, they may choose to avoid being set up for a bidding war.

  - List at market:

    - Pro: You may also be able to get a bidding war going with this pricing strategy.

    - Con: There's not much of a con here, except that you might not attract as many buyers into making an offer.

  - List above market:

    - Pro: This will eliminate tire kickers and wishful thinkers who think they can afford a property that they really can't.

    - Con: You may miss out on an ideal buyer who is turned off by the high price and will not go to the effort of presenting a lower and more realistic offer.

- Average property in average condition, with average finishes. You have two logical choices:

- List at market:

  - Pro: You should be able to defend this price relatively well, because you can back it up with valid comparables when listing at market value.

  - Con: You may not get many people making offers at asking price, so you'll have your work cut out for you to bring them up.

- List above market:

  - Pro: This will eliminate tire kickers and wishful thinkers who think they can afford a property that they really can't.

  - Con: You may miss out on an ideal buyer who is turned off by the high price and will not go to the effort of presenting a lower and more realistic offer.

- Less desirable property, perhaps needing a lot of work, or in a bad area. The two pricing options I would normally choose from are:

  - List below market:

    - Pro: This will certainly get you offers.

    - Con: Some people may be scared off by the "it's too good to be true" feeling of the situation, and when you do get offers, the buyers will have a million points they can use to argue on keeping the price very low.

  - List at market:

    - Pro: You should somewhat be able to defend your asking price.

    - Con: You may not get too much interest, because most people looking at this type of property are really looking for a deal.

- Many similar properties are for sale on the same street, in a certain neighbourhood, or in a condo building:

  - List below market. You may want to do this if this property is average or less desirable:

    - Pro: Your listing will likely get lots of attention.

    - Con: When buyers realize that you're just using a low price as a lure to focus their attention on your property and away from other properties they can buy, they'll likely turn to the other properties to start fresh negotiations.

- List at market. This choice could be used if this property is attractive, average, or less desirable:

  - Pro: You are being honest right off the bat, and you'll likely position your listing in the middle of the pack. Use other things to get buyers' attention, like a large variety of quality pictures, good staging, virtual tours, and higher commission (this will get the attention of the buyers' agents).

  - Con: You are going to be in the middle of the pack of properties for sale, so the lower priced ones or better packaged ones will likely get more attention.

- List above market. I would only go this route if this property is attractive or average:

  - Pro: You may be able to get buyers to think there is something special about your property, but this is unlikely, unless something truly does set it apart from the rest, such as a special feature, an exceptional view, something extra included in the sale, and so on.

  - Con: If there are lots of other similar properties available nearby, most buyers will check those out too. You're likely going to be trying to convince your client to lower the asking price.

Keep in mind that even within each pricing strategy above, you have a lot of leeway. For example, if your aim is to price a property under market in order to garner a lot of attention, you can price it 2%–5% under market, or 10% under market. Each of these scenarios will achieve more, or less, of the pros and cons I've listed. Additionally, if you have a prospective listing in an area with lots of similar properties for sale, you likely have to also take into account whether it is a gem, average, or below average. Other pricing situations can be even more complicated. Hopefully you can now see why I say that real estate brokerage and negotiations are part art, part experience, and part knowledge.

Motivating a Seller to Accept an Offer

The work required to convince a seller to accept a reasonable offer starts much earlier than the negotiation stage. It is imperative that, first, the asking price and bottom price your client thinks he or she will accept are realistic, and second, that you continually condition your client along the sales cycle. For example, say you have established that your listing needs to be priced slightly above market to allow for negotiations, and after several showings, the feedback from potential buyers' realtors is that the house seems a little run down. Your job is to let your client know, in a diplomatic way, that if a decent offer doesn't materialize soon, he may want to consider doing a little bit of work and perhaps a paint job to spruce the house up, or he should be ready for buyers to ask for a slightly lower price to allow for the cost and time it will take them to do so themselves.

I recently assisted a new client whom I met when she took my commercial real estate investing course at the University of Toronto. She had bought a residential condo pre-construction as an investment, and then rented it out when she took possession of it. She decided it was time to sell, because it had likely appreciated by close to $100,000 above what she had paid originally. I listed the property, but we had problems with the tenant, who did not make much of an effort to present the unit in its best light. Once the tenant left, my client agreed to pay to have the unit cleaned properly, but she decided not to have it staged. Because it had been lingering on the market for some time, she agreed to a price reduction, and then to a second one. My client explained to me that she didn't want to have to deal with residential tenants anymore, and was eager to buy her first commercial investment property, but needed the funds from the condo sale to purchase a commercial property. I went over the costs involved in carrying an empty condo unit for several more months—mortgage interest, utilities, condo fees, property taxes, and so on—and she was primed to negotiate reasonably with any offer that came in. Finally, an offer did come in, and although we worked the purchase price up over several rounds of sign backs, she ended up accepting far less than she had originally thought she would.

It is critical to show a client how and why you have come up with a suggested selling price (or, often better, suggest a range; for example, $500,000–$530,000). An asking price (or your suggested selling price) should, almost always, be arrived at by using quality comparables. "Quality" means that the comparables are as recent as possible, are for properties as geographically similar as possible, and, of course, as mentioned in Chapter 1, are for properties that have actually sold—not currently-for-sale, or expired listings.

It is important to put the subject property into geographic perspective, outside of looking at comparables. This allows your clients to understand the situation and the parameters you are working within. If, for example, the subject property is very close to a shopping centre, but everyone drives there, it would not be valid for your client to say that the subject property is a block closer to the shopping centre than many other properties on the market, and therefore it should be worth more. Another example is when the subject property is just barely on the "wrong side of the tracks." You and your client can't do anything about this, and that border may be somewhat blurry, but at the end of the day, if public perception is "wrong side of the tracks," then that is the reality you have to work with. It doesn't mean the property won't sell, but comparables one street over, on the "right side of the tracks," may not be relevant.

There are times when you may have to ask for guidance from a realtor who knows an area particularly well. For example, Patrick Rocca is a realtor who specializes in the Leaside neighbourhood in Toronto. He advertises prominently throughout the area, and has so many listings that you cannot help but know his name simply by driving through the Leaside area, because his name is on all his for-sale signs. This is powerful branding at work, and he has made a name for himself using this method.

However, geographic specialization—or geo-farming—does not appeal to all realtors, and it does not suit some realtors' personalities. If you don't know an area well but would like confirmation of your pricing strategy for a listing, don't hesitate to call a local real estate expert. In my experience, if you approach them kindly and with respect, most realtors don't have a problem sharing their knowledge for a few minutes. Short-sighted individuals may think they are helping their competition—but consider that the agent calling you already has the listing, or is about to get it, and by helping the other agent, you can always call on her for a favour down the road. In addition, many successful realtors know many other agents quite well, and when they pool their knowledge and compare their experiences, they are all able to provide better service to their clients.

For example, you could call a local expert and explain to him that you are about to list a semi-detached home on a 45-by-120-foot lot, which is very similar to 123 Main Street and 456 Middle Road (properties in his area), and you'd appreciate his input on whether the selling prices in the last three to six months have been stable for comparable properties (this helps you in determining whether you can give proper weight to these comparables). At the same time, you could also ask the local agent whether he typically has buyers for this type of property, and if he likes to be kept informed when you list the property, or likes to receive marketing materials and information.

The more you specialize and are familiar with a particular neighbourhood, the easier it is to accurately price a property. Get a feel for other listings in the neighbourhood. View listings for competitor properties, with or without your clients. This is often done when you start looking for comparables, but remember that a comparable is only truly applicable if it has sold. When you do your search for comparables, also check into what is available on the market that could appeal to potential buyers of your listing. This could be the majority of the properties in the same neighbour-hood, but, depending on the product (for example, $2-million-plus homes), you may find properties in a large area that are in the same price range that might be competition for your listing. Once you have a good inventory of competitive properties, review the listings carefully, looking at any photos that are available. If you feel there are a few houses that are very real competition, you may even want to go visit them, because buyers and realtors will likely refer to them when discussing your listing, or when negotiating an offer with you.

•   •   •

You and the seller have agreed on an asking price for her property, and you now need to recommend what needs to be done to her property to achieve her desired price. The information in Chapter 6 may be useful when discussing an asking price with the seller, because investing a little money preparing the property for sale can often result in a higher sale price.

Preparing a Home for Sale

Once you have a listing, you need to reflect on what advice to give to your client with respect to preparing his or her home for sale. There are several factors that need to be considered, not the least of which are time and money. Some of these are common sense, such as having a well-maintained yard in the spring, summer, and fall and a shovelled and salted driveway, walkway, and front steps in the winter. Others are more judgment calls, such as replacing a functional but old central air conditioning system, or painting the interior walls of the home in a neutral colour. The main context for deciding what to do is the client's goal and wishes. Is a fast sale desirable and as important as the selling price? Or is the client not in any particular hurry? The client looks to you for guidance.

Home Staging

Home staging is the act of preparing a residential property for sale, to make it appear as attractive as possible to the widest range of buyer profiles. In most cases, a staged home increases the perceived value of a property and generates a higher asking price. Homes that have been staged are often classified as "move-in ready," which, depending on the property, can be appealing to the average family, given the modern hectic lifestyles many of us lead. Not many people have the time to renovate or even plan to renovate, nor do they want to create more work than they might already see that a property requires.

While home staging has been a marketing tool for many years, until fairly recently it was mostly evident in new residential and condominium developments to showcase the model homes and condo units that were used to give potential buyers a sense of what their home could look like.

By creating an attractive living space that emphasized the home's features and functionality according to the target market, a desire to live within the subdivision or the condo building was created. Doing so dramatically assisted in the sale of the properties.

The impact that home staging has on days on market (DOM) is clear from these statistics from the Real Estate Staging Association (RESA) in 2009:

- Vacant homes:

  - Unstaged: Average 277 DOM

  - Staged and re-listed: Average 63 DOM (78 percent less time on market)

- Occupied homes:

  - Unstaged: Average 233 DOM

  - Staged and re-listed: Average 53 DOM (78 percent less time on market)

- Not previously on the market:

  - Staged (vacant and occupied) homes: Average 40.5 DOM

The process of staging can vary depending on each situation, but in general it is the process of:

- **Depersonalizing a living space:** This includes removing personal items such as photographs, artwork, sports trophies and awards, and other memorabilia. You want people walking through to imagine a house as their home, not feel as if they are walking through somebody else's.

- **De-cluttering:** We all have *stuff*, and that stuff can create the illusion of a smaller room, closet, or cupboard. It also leaves a property looking messy, to the detriment of the property as a whole. Have the client pack up any items that won't be needed for the next three months, and store unnecessary items and furniture. An added benefit of this de-cluttering and cleanup is that it will drastically assist in the moving process once the property is sold and the sellers must move.

- **Reorganizing:** This means creating the highest and best use for every room. Although a spare room might currently work well as a home gym for the seller, potential buyers might question whether or not the size is sufficient for a bed. By staging that room with a small bed and reasonably-sized furniture, potential buyers can imagine using that space.

- **Neutralizing:** This fits hand in hand with depersonalizing. Neutral colours are generally most appealing when it comes to the sale of a home. They are important in order to create a generic space, where anyone can picture any potential use—one that is attractive to the highest number of potential buyers. If the seller has floral wallpaper or an overly bright colour in the family room, for example, it could be off-putting to a potential buyer (although some buyers are capable of visualizing a room with a different colour or wall treatment).

- **Cleaning and making repairs:** Depending on the home, this can range dramatically from fixing chipped paint and a leaky faucet, to putting down new laminate flooring and replacing a kitchen counter, to upgrading hardware, just to name a few. Anything broken or in need of repair is seen as "work" and "more cost" in a buyer's eyes. Cleaning a home is also essential to the sale; not many buyers meet an asking price for a property in an unsanitary state.

Buyers are very judgmental when it comes to purchasing residential real estate. The purchase of a home is the largest investment most individuals will ever make, so they have every right to be critical. It has become more important than ever for sellers to eliminate any negative aspect of the property that they intend to sell, because buyers are more sophisticated and informed, and have greater access to information than they did a few decades ago. They are very aware when a specific property is lacking, and either pass it over or adjust their offering price accordingly.

From the minute a potential buyer walks up to the front door, curb appeal plays a huge role. A manicured lawn and beautiful flowers in the garden leave a lasting impression. But so does a screen door that's shot full of holes. The first impression sets the mindset of the buyer, and that mindset can carry over to the interior. If a potential buyer is greeted with a clean, airy home in good repair, a positive impression will last through the duration of his inspecting the home.

However, if there are mysterious and unpleasant odours, cracks in the drywall, or a generally untidy appearance, a negative impression will be formed that will carry through the rest of the tour of the property and negatives will outweigh any positives.

There are various levels of staging that are appropriate for all budgets and every type of situation (sometimes all that is needed is a fresh coat of paint or the reorganization of storage space, like, for example, cupboards and closets):

- **Using what the seller has in her possession:** This is the most cost-effective way to stage a home, and where appropriate, it's the most flattering to the seller, because you can use her own furnishings and decor to show each space in its best light. It is not uncommon, however, for a home stager to suggest minor upgrades such as paint and hardware at an additional cost to the seller.

- **Renting furniture:** In instances where the home value surpasses the visual value of the furniture, furniture can be rented on a piece-by-piece or month-to-month basis, specifically for home-staging purposes. Renting furniture can completely change the visual flow of any property and can help transform old spaces into modern masterpieces.

  It is more common now to stage vacant properties, whether just the main living and selling areas (master bedroom, kitchen, and family room) or the whole home. Vacant properties can be difficult to sell and often result in a lower asking price. The reason for this, generally, is that people have a hard time imagining how a room flows, if a couch will fit, or how furniture will fit in an odd-shaped room. By placing furniture in the house, the potential buyer will have a better idea of the home's livability.

- **Making extensive repairs:** In some cases, it is necessary to make repairs and upgrades to bring a property up to code—or even to make it sellable. Whether a complete kitchen renovation, upgraded carpets, or a bathroom renovation, changes generate a higher asking price and give the property added value.

A few years ago, I listed a new client's property in a market that was not particularly weak, but neither was it very strong. When I gave him the price range I thought the property could realistically be sold for, the price to list as-is, and the list price if he spent a few thousand dollars preparing the house for sale, this client chose to invest no money, but insisted on listing at a higher price than I thought was wise. In this scenario, I often tell my clients that I cannot work on their property at that price, but this particular seller agreed to revisit the price in two weeks if there were no serious offers. As you have no doubt guessed, two weeks later he and I were having coffee to discuss the lack of offers and the negative comments from realtors who had shown the house to their clients. All of the feedback indicated that we were priced quite a bit too high—to the point that buyers were not even interested in making low offers.

I told this client, as gently as possible, that if he didn't want to follow my advice, I would cancel the listing agreement. Finally, he agreed to spend a few thousand dollars on extensive staging assistance (which included a great deal of furniture, as my client's was very dated and in poor condition), and also to spend $2,000 more on touch-up repairs, some painting, and a very thorough cleaning. A week after the new listing was posted on MLS, along with the post-staging pictures and a virtual tour, a firm offer was negotiated that was about $10,000 higher than other comparable properties had sold for in the area.

Should You Consider Being Certified as a Home Stager?

Over the past 10–15 years, staging has become more and more common, and, in many cases, essential to the sale of residential properties. Residential realtors now often offer it as a value-added free service as part of their listing packages in order to further appeal to potential sellers.

If this fits with your business model, you might consider becoming a certified home stager. Since home-staging certification isn't a regulated profession, anyone can practise home staging with or without the designation. However, it is often beneficial to obtain the certification, as consumers will often look for some sort of indication that shows the home stager is qualified to perform the work being offered.

Home staging is often offered through an established home-staging practice. Courses can be designed to fit one's schedule. Some topics covered in a course include performing a staging evaluation, establishing balance, creating a visual flow, choosing colour combinations and making recommendations, de-cluttering, learning style types, suggesting changes, relating with customers, and exploring suggested staging practices and business practices.

Associations related to home staging in Canada include the Real Estate Staging Association (RESA), which is established throughout North America and has five chapters serving the Greater Toronto Area. Members of this association receive resources, guidance, training, and special designation. RESA also offers information to the consumer relating to the home-staging industry, including statistics, what to look for when hiring a home stager, and a list of the association's members.

Realtors looking to find additional information on staging can go to RESA; they can in turn provide this information to their clients. The

International Association of Home Staging Professionals (IAHSP), which has a regional chapter in Toronto (the Toronto GTA Staging Association, or TGTASA), is another resource for GTA stagers. Though much smaller than RESA, it does provide a variety of resources for stagers.

• • •

You have a listing. You've advised your client on what he can do to help sell his property faster and for more money. Now you need to market the listing, which involves some of the same channels you use to market yourself as a realtor, both of which I cover in Chapter 7.

Using Digital Tools for Branding and Marketing

The use of social media tools is critical and widespread across many industries and professions. Real estate is no exception.

Digital Media

Living in North America today, you cannot deny the impact of digital media and its penetration into our lives. Realtors need to assess digital media tools in order to best determine where to spend time and money marketing listings and promoting their brand.

Smartphones and other mobile devices make up one of the fastest-growing digital media market segments, and represent opportunities for forward-thinking real estate agents. Here are a few points to consider:

- Consumers spend 10 percent of their media attention on their mobile devices, but the medium commands a mere 1 percent of the total amount of advertising dollars spent.

- The print medium is quickly becoming anachronistic for several reasons, including cost, oversaturation in the eyes of consumers, and a limited audience.

- More than two-thirds of the time people spend on mobile phones is now used for non-communication activities (in other words, looking for content).

- The average American spends 90-plus minutes per day utilizing mobile apps versus 72 minutes on web-based consumption (although this is a U.S. statistic, we can draw parallels in the Great White North).

- Mobile devices are poised to surpass television as the dominant consumer access point for all media.

Digital Photographs

According to the National Association of Realtors (again, an American organization, but from my experience, their numbers are close to reality in Canada), approximately 15 percent of agents use professional photography to market their listings. The use of professional photographers is not more widespread because agents are reluctant to add additional up-front costs to their marketing plans. Such costs may be money poorly spent if the realtor is trying to move a property quickly. But again, the comparables in the area must be taken into consideration and treated as competition. Can you get a higher price with a small up-front investment? Here are some creative ways to mitigate the investment in professional photography:

- Ask the client to pay for the photography. You may want to wait until you have a listing agreement signed before you explore this idea, in case this suggestion rubs the client the wrong way.

- Explain that studies[1] show that properties listed with professional photography sell for more money, and propose that the client pay for having this done up front; however, when you sell the property, the cost for the photographer comes out of your commission.

  This is a no-risk proposition for the realtor. If you sell the property, bingo! Who cares if you paid for the photography? You have a commission in your pocket. If you don't sell the property, sure, you've spent some time on it, but you aren't out of pocket for the photography (and the photographs belong to the sellers and allow them to eventually sell their property anyway).

According to a recent survey of buyers and sellers by the National Association of Realtors, 80 percent of buyers used the Internet while researching their real estate purchase. These buyers rated photographs as the single most useful tool in their search of properties on the market.

---

[1] Evidence that properties listed with professional photography sell for more money:

http://photographyforrealestate.net/2012/06/12/professional-real-estate-photos-are-worth-anywhere-from-1000-to-116000-in-a-home-sale/

See point #4: http://bhgrealestateblog.com/2012/08/01/8-reasons-why-you-should-consider-using-a-professional-photographer/

http://www.picturesdosellhouses.com/wp-content/uploads/2010/08/mls-average.jpg

One study compared the number of photos in a listing to the number of days it took to sell the listed property. The study showed that listings with more photos sold faster. Here are the results:

- 1 photo = 70 days on market (DOM)
- 6 photos = 40 DOM
- 16–19 photos = 36 DOM
- 20 photos max = 32 DOM

Another interesting result from this study was that listings with fewer photos sold for less than the original asking price:

- 1 photo = 91.2% of original price
- 6 or more = 95% of original price

To put this into dollars so that it can easily be understood, here is an example: A $600,000 home could sell for as much as 3.8% ($22,000) *less*, if it is shown with only one photo. In the study, only 12 percent of agents posted the maximum number allowed—20 photos.

According to a National Association of Realtors survey on the web of what buyers found "very useful," 83 percent said photos were the most useful, followed by comprehensive detail about the property (81 percent) and virtual tours (60 percent).

Having professional photos taken makes sense even for lower-end properties. One Toronto agent, Richard Silver, said that after using professional photographers for two years, his sales had gone up about 25 percent. He commented: "I don't even put out a listing without professional photos."

Social Media

The number of popular social media platforms has soared in recent years, and they now allow users to post text, images, videos, and links very easily. If you already have a large social media presence, you can drive considerable traffic to your website just using your social media accounts, which is a ridiculously economical way of generating hits on your website.

The popular social network Facebook, for example, had over 800 million users as of May 2012. Imagine if only a small percentage of Facebook users who live in the area you serve visited your website because they are interested in buying or selling real estate. Now you can image the potential that social media presents to a realtor today.

Here is a short list of what social media can do for you and your business:

- Drive traffic to your website and online listings.

- Drive traffic to your open houses and other properties.

- Help develop your personal and agency brands.

- Connect you with new customers and help you remain connected to your previous customers.

- Connect you with other realtors and brokerages to broaden your business network, increasing partnership opportunities (and as I discuss in Chapter 3, affording you opportunities, through this business network, to find properties you wouldn't have been exposed to otherwise, and to sell or lease your listings faster).

Social Media Branding

The image you project across your social media platforms must be authentic or you will lose your audience by virtue of your message becoming diluted or confusing. It is vital to have a cohesive brand and voice to get the most out of your social media presence. They should be extensions of a clearly defined brand message and answer the following questions:

- Who are you?

- What do you do?

- With whom do you want to have a conversation?

- Why should your network or community care about your message?

- What do you want to accomplish with Twitter? Facebook? LinkedIn?

A realtor's or brokerage's brand voice should reflect the personality traits of the brand. For example, if you want your real estate brand persona to be perceived as personable and results-driven, you must use language in your social media activities that underpins that persona. I do not mean being boastful or over-promising. Choose your words carefully to suggest you are a dynamic and experienced realtor with people skills.

It is a good idea to develop an idea of your brand tone (for example, boisterous, bold, personal, humble, or professional), but be careful that you don't try to adopt a tone that is not authentic. I choose my language very carefully to reflect who I am and what values I stand for.

One way to help you create a social media brand is to create a quadrant with the headings "brand," "language," "tone," and "purpose." Write down aspects of each of these points in the quadrant; this will help you focus your social media message to best support your brand and reinforce what you'd like to achieve with online networks.

Social Media Strategy

Creating a social media road map and timetable is very important, because it helps guide your account development. Scheduling your use of social media makes execution easier and increases the value of your social media presence. For example, make a schedule that includes blogging on Tuesdays and Thursdays, and commit to tweeting every Monday, Wednesday, and Friday.

As you start to explore the social media landscape and you flesh out your personality in this environment, make sure to actively retweet, #hashtag, and @mention other users to engage in conversation that will drive your exposure and make followers more comfortable engaging with you online.

The following sections are dedicated to the most influential and well-known social media networks today, which have shown the most promise in giving realtors a platform to attract new and repeat clients.

Twitter

Twitter is a great way to keep connected to previous customers, the real estate industry, and other followers in general. Here are some basic Twitter facts to get you up and running:

- It is the SMS (text messaging) of the Internet to the world.

- It makes you the point of broadcast. There is no need to use other networks to spread your message.

- It provides instant communication.

- It is driven by 140-character messages (tweets), which include web-linking abilities (links to web pages, images, and other Twitter accounts).

- It should be viewed as an open conversation that can evolve in different ways.

- The website address is: twitter.com.

- If you'd like to search for content, visit: search.twitter.com.

- It is an easy way to send your new listings out to the market so that anyone can see them.

Here are some Twitter terms, in case you're not already neck-deep in this world:

- **Tweet:** A message sent on Twitter. For example: "New 4-bedroom home on Post Road going for $4,599,000. Contact @claudeboiron #luxury #Toronto."

- **Follow:** Following another user's tweets in your account. When they send messages out you can view them as part of your aggregated follow list.

- **Follower:** Someone who follows you by subscribing to your tweets. The more followers you have, the greater your network reach.

- **Mention:** Mentioning another user account in a tweet by using an @ symbol in front of it, such as the "@claudeboiron" in the tweet above. If you are mentioned, you show up in others' messages, and that increases your visibility to their viewers and followers. The more you're mentioned, the more followers you get, and the more exposure for your brand. When you reply to someone, you mention them.

- **Retweet:** When a tweet is re-posted to another account that it did not originate from. If you create compelling content, this is a phenomenon that you experience, and it allows your message to reach an exponentially larger audience.

If you're not sold yet, for your curiosity or interest, here are some Twitter statistics from a March 2011 report from Sysomos:

- **3 years, 2 months, and 1 day:** The time that elapsed between the first tweet and the billionth tweet.

- **1 week:** The time it now takes for users to send a billion tweets.

- **50 million:** The average number of tweets people sent per day in March 2010.

- **140 million:** The average number of tweets people sent per day in February 2011.

- **177 million:** Tweets sent on March 11, 2011.

- **456:** Tweets per second (TPS) when Michael Jackson died on June 25, 2009—a record at that time.

- **572,000:** Number of new Twitter accounts created on March 12, 2011.

- **460,000:** Average number of new Twitter accounts per day over February 2011.

- **182 percent:** Increase in number of mobile Twitter users over the year 2011.

- **8, 29, 130, 350, 400:** Number of Twitter employees in January 2008, January 2009, January 2010, January 2011, and March 2012 respectively.

- **71 percent:** Proportion of tweets that get no reaction.

- **6 percent:** Proportion of tweets that are retweeted.

- **92 percent:** Proportion of those tweets that are retweeted within an hour.

- **1.63 percent:** Proportion of retweets that happen in the second hour after submission.

- **0.94 percent:** Proportion of retweets that take place in the third hour after submission.

- **48 hours:** Amount of time from submission in which almost all retweets take place.

- **96.9 percent:** Proportion of replies that occur within the first hour of the original tweet.

- **0.88 percent:** Proportion of replies that happen in the second hour; after that, replies drop off dramatically.

Facebook

Your real estate audience has mostly moved from bench and newspaper ads, bus shelter posters, and coffee shop message board postings, and it's a good idea to have a Facebook page that represents you, your expertise, and your listings. (If you don't use a personal Facebook profile to interact much socially, you may be able to use it for your real estate career instead of a page, though this is not as desirable professionally).

To help you appreciate your potential market, consider this statistic: there are 6.7 million Facebook users above the age of 18 in Ontario who declare their location (based on a June 2012 search of Facebook). The average Facebook user is comfortable with the Internet and starts many of his purchasing decisions online.

If you're not familiar with Facebook yet, you should know that Facebook is a very comfortable online experience for people who use it for discovery and sharing. This no-pressure experience can be very valuable to you as consumers become increasingly informed and have less tolerance for blatant sales approaches. Here are some facts about Facebook from its website:

- The average Facebook visit time is 20 minutes.

- 60 percent of Facebook users are aged 35 and older.

- Facebook became the number one ranked website in the United States on March 9, 2010.

- "Facebook" is the term most searched for in Canada, and Facebook-related queries account for 14 percent of the top search-result clicks.

- The Facebook fan base is loyal and spends a significant portion of their online time on the Facebook site.

LinkedIn

This professional-development and networking site has experienced incredible growth in its first 10 years of existence. Originally developed as a site for people to network professionally, especially for employment purposes, it has grown to be much more than that, including being a great sales platform for salespeople and a great audience for advertising.

Here are some LinkedIn facts (from their website, www.linkedin.com), in case you're not aware of how much importance this network has in Canada's professional community:

- LinkedIn started out in the living room of co-founder Reid Hoffman in 2002.

- The site officially launched on May 5, 2003. At the end of its first month in operation, LinkedIn had a total of 4,500 members in the network.

- On March 31, 2012 (the end of the first quarter), professionals were signing up to join LinkedIn at a rate of approximately two new members per second.

- The company is publicly held and has a diversified business model with revenues coming from hiring solutions, marketing solutions, and premium subscriptions.

- As of March 31, 2012, LinkedIn operates the world's largest professional network on the Internet, with 161 million members in over 200 countries and territories.

- LinkedIn members did nearly 4.2 billion professionally oriented searches on the platform in 2011 and were on pace to surpass 5.3 billion in 2012.

- LinkedIn is currently available in 17 languages: English, Czech, Dutch, French, German, Indonesian, Italian, Japanese, Korean, Malay, Polish, Portuguese, Romanian, Russian, Spanish, Swedish, and Turkish.

- It has 5-million-plus members in Canada as of January 19, 2012.

- More than 2 million companies have LinkedIn company pages.

- LinkedIn represents a valuable demographic for marketers with an affluent and influential membership.

- As of March 31, 2012, there are more than 400,000 unique domains actively using the LinkedIn share button on their sites to send content to the LinkedIn platform.

- LinkedIn members are sharing insights and knowledge in more than 1 million LinkedIn groups.

- In the last week of March 2012, 22 percent of unique visiting members came from mobile devices.

Not only does LinkedIn offer great sales and advertising opportunities, but it allows you to build an intuitive-to-view professional résumé, with details on any positions you've held, awards you've earned, education details, languages you speak, specializations you've pursued, publications you've written, and courses or seminars you've given. Additionally, LinkedIn enables the creation of groups of LinkedIn members, which can be open or restricted, where members can ask questions of each other, comment, or make suggestions.

Strategically joining LinkedIn and starting some groups, and contributing material and knowledge of value, allows you to showcase yourself as an expert in your industry, property type, or neighbourhood.

Realtor Websites

You have so many options today when deciding on the type of website you'd like to present to the world. Obviously, you can develop and manage your own, but unless you are seriously talented in IT, online marketing, and search engine optimization (SEO), as well as graphic artistry and web coding, you should probably consider asking experts to assist you in this crucial element of your real estate career.

Although I'm not specifically recommending any realtor website providers, here are a few that offer varying degrees of support and services. Speaking with one or all of them, or simply visiting their websites, should get you thinking about the various elements that need to go into a website to suit your professional needs.

- **Real Web Solutions** (www.realwebsolutions.com): These folks are probably the foremost used by real estate agents in the Greater Toronto Area. They offer templates for building a website to brokerages and real estate companies. The company also does custom work. It also includes its own customer relationship management software (CRM). You must host your website on its servers.

- **Real Estate Web Masters** (www.realestatewebmasters.com): This company does sites for agents, brokerages, and custom Internet data exchange (IDX) feeds. Based in Nanaimo, B.C., its services start at around $2,500 for design, and many of the pieces use proprietary technology. You must host your website on its servers.

- **Corefuel** (www.corefuel.com): The company is located in Toronto and it has, for example, designed the website for Otto Calta (www.thinktorontohomes.com). It has also listed a number of real estate websites in its portfolio (see www.liveinto.ca and www.north yorkcondos.ca).

Search Engine Optimization (SEO)

SEO is an acronym you hear a lot these days. Whether you offer goods or services online or in person, and your product is discount or luxury,

SEO affects you if you have a website or if you are listed on other websites. Websites receive views through a combination of traffic sources: direct (from email links or business cards), referral (Facebook, Twitter, and other websites), and search engines (Google, Bing, Yahoo!, and so on).

Technically speaking, SEO is optimizing a website for visibility on search engines, the result of which is driving traffic to your site. It is essential that you are using SEO for your real estate website if you rely on it to generate leads for your business. Otherwise, your website can really be called an expensive business card or résumé, because people will mostly find your site only from typing in the URL from your business card, from advertising, and from real estate signs.

If you want to show up in search results in Google, Bing, and Yahoo!, you need to work on your SEO. Search engines index or record information about your site in a specific way and do their best to connect your page to the rest of the Internet with links, visit information, and your written and displayed website content. Search engines try to understand the importance of your site in relation to the specific search criteria. If you type "realtor" into a search engine, do you want a definition, or do you want to find someone who can help you with your property needs near your location?

The way you structure your website links and content affect how search engines view your importance or relevance. The trick is to create pages that are built for human visitors to your site as well as for search engines. When creating titles for your pages, be mindful of length, place important keywords close to the front, insert your brand name, and consider readability and emotional impact. A successful SEO strategy can lead to lots of business being generated for you automatically (in other words, invest in a good SEO plan initially, and you may be able to get away with paying only a nominal monthly rate to keep the SEO gravy continuing). Many people and organizations have built their businesses solely on search-engine-generated traffic.

Researching Keywords

When you first create, and later promote, your real estate website, it is vital that you pick valuable keywords or keyword phrases. Google Keyword Tool is a great website to help you to not only check out the competition for each of your desired keywords, but also to determine how many searches each keyword receives, both locally and globally. This research can help you tailor your keywords to your desired audience while also increasing your chances of success in marketing these keywords.

Using Keywords in Titles

SEO experts say that they cannot emphasize enough how essential it is that you use your keywords effectively. Here are some tips for doing so:

- When creating titles for everything from your website pages to your blog posts and URL links, you should include your keywords in the titles. As a result, search engines are more likely to pick up on your keywords and move your site to the top of the page.

- When you create blog posts or pages for your website that are related to other content on your website, include an internal link back to other blog posts or website pages. For example: "You should definitely check out our tips on getting the best mortgage rates." The underlined section would be a hyperlink to a blog or post you created about tips on getting the best mortgage rates. Utilizing this strategy results in keeping viewers in your content streams (on your website) and helps with SEO.

Continuing to Write More Content

One trap that many people fall into is spending more time than is necessary creating relevant content for their website and achieving the desired ranking, but then stopping all their efforts. In a matter of weeks after they stop creating new content, they slip in the search engine rankings. Keeping your website updated with fresh content is important for effective real estate SEO. Writing blog and website content gives you and your team an opportunity to actively review and reinforce your brand, approach, language, and presentation of your business. By writing about what you do and what you know on a regular basis, you're forced to reflect on how to optimize your sales and marketing strategies, while building trust in your viewers that you really know what you're talking about. Asking your staff to review their processes and write content for your marketing activities will also require them to reflect on their knowledge and daily work activities, which can also bring operational efficiencies and internal growth to your business that you might not have thought possible otherwise.

Including Images

Using images in real estate SEO is extremely important because real estate is an image-oriented industry. The most recent Google algorithm changes in 2012 seem to indicate that original images and other media are being weighed more heavily than ever before in the battle for top search results. Properly structured, image embedding and linking can help your SEO strategy and drive traffic to your site—but using this technology is above my head, and perhaps yours, which is why using a SEO expert may be a good idea. If you are doing it all yourself, make sure you put a description of the image and a URL that includes one of your targeted keywords or key phrases. Always keep in mind that search engines like images and a clear idea of what they are.

Getting External Links

Try to get your site link posted on other blogs or related websites. Stay away from free back-linking services, as they can hurt your rank with the search engines. Be patient. If you are employing a proper real estate SEO strategy, your website will start climbing in rank and driving more traffic, leads, and sales.

Integrating Social Media

When you create or update blog posts for web pages or for your own real estate website, make sure you let your clients, friends, and industry contacts know, using your social media networks. This will remind them of your business and provide you with possible feedback that can help you structure your marketing literature for your business. A common way of doing this is to use a social media button, which, with one click, allows you or your readers to "Send to Facebook," "Tweet This," "Send to LinkedIn," and so on.

Other Advertising and Marketing

I don't spend too much time on this section because these forms of advertising and marketing have been around for a very long time, but I should remind you that some of these options are still valid methods to market yourself and your properties:

- Newspaper ads
- Bench ads
- Public transportation ads (bus shelters, buses, streetcars, and subway cars)
- Digital and poster displays in restaurants, public areas, washrooms, taxis, and so on

- You: you are probably the most effective form of advertisement and marketing, since you know what you are talking about, and you have the opportunity, many times each day, to make a positive impact on the people you interact with

· · ·

Once you've found a client who wants to list a property with you, you need to get ready to guide her through the process of selling—from preparing her property for sale to putting it on the market, and from hosting open houses to dealing with offers when they come in. I cover all of this, including how to best work with other realtors, in Chapter 8.

From Showing to Offer

Working with Other Realtors

Realtors would love to double-end many, if not all, of their deals. The reality is, however, that as a listing agent, you are very dependent on other realtors to show your listing to their buyer clients, and bring them to the table with an offer. It is therefore important for you to be helpful and responsive to other agents. This process of working with other agents begins when you prepare the listing documentation and the MLS paperwork. Make sure you fill it all out as completely as possible. Ask your clients questions about their property, and if they don't have the answers, try to find the answers for them. For example, if you're selling a house on a large piece of land that is directly in the path of development, you should contact the local planning department to find out what the development potential is for the property, and what restrictions or requirements might be involved. Include as many pictures as possible and any useful additional documents such as floor plans, a survey, and a detailed description of the property and surrounding area.

If an agent calls to ask you questions about your listing (I often do this as soon as my buyer clients show interest in a given property, since there is always more to learn from the listing agent, because many details are not mentioned in the listing), give him as much of your time as he needs. The agent is trying to sell your listing, which will, in the end, make you money, so be patient and helpful. A pet peeve I have is when listing agents don't provide their cell phone number on their listings (although I do understand the reason for this with female realtors). In some cases, this may be the policy of the brokerage. However, I would discuss this point with your brokerage. I'm a pit bull when it comes to getting information or answers for my clients, but I've had to give up a few times when it was virtually impossible to get in touch with the listing agent. If your brokerage tells callers or other agents they're not allowed to give out agents' cell numbers, explain to your manager or the broker of record that this practice is limiting your ability to make sales. My partner often says that businesspeople must strike while the iron is hot. I agree with this idiom. If an agent's buyer client is interested in a property, you want the agent to get answers quickly, so that she can cultivate that interest, not lose it by failing to find out the information she needs.

Make it easy for other agents to work with you. For example, most realtors now deal with offers via email, but some holdouts do not. It is imperative that you have a smartphone so you can respond quickly to any inquiries you receive. Ensure that buyers and other agents can easily find your email address on your website. It may be tempting to have visitors to your website fill out a contact form so you can add them to your database, but make sure you include your email address outside that form. Recently, I was on another agent's website because a client wanted to see one of her listings. When I called the brokerage to book the showing for Saturday afternoon, I discovered they were closed for the week and, uncharacteristically, they did not have an answering service to take calls outside of business hours. When I went online, I was pleasantly surprised to find that the listing agent had a function on her website that allowed me to download her contact information in different formats. I was able to download her contact card on my smartphone, but when I opened it, there was no cell phone number or email address! I had to do more digging, but I finally found her email address and was finally able to request a showing.

Holding an Open House

Open-house strategies can vary, depending on the property you have for sale (very desirable, average, or difficult to sell). It is a good rule of thumb to put the property on the MLS on a Wednesday or Thursday. This way, the listing will go out in agents' pre-programmed MLS searches to their buyer clients the following morning, and will populate the public MLS website the following day, allowing buyers and their realtors to plan on visiting your open house on the weekend or to book showings. Make sure you've programmed the weekend open house or open houses you'll be hosting.

Open-house signs should be distributed over the neighbourhood on Friday night or Saturday morning, with the goal of drawing visitors from main arteries down to the side streets your listing is on (if applicable), or into the condo building in question. The signs should have all of the mandatory brokerage information, but also include the property address, the date and time of the open house, as well as some information to pique view-ers' interest, such as "huge lot, 5BR," or "4BR, 3WR, under $450K," or "2BR, lowest condo fees," and so on.

During the open house itself, you should be present and the sellers should not. If you absolutely cannot be there, recruit a knowledgeable and reliable colleague from your brokerage, and make sure you tell her enough about the property so that she can intelligently answer questions. You should also have colour property brochures available for visitors to take with them. Hopefully you've worked with your clients to prepare the property for sale, and it shows in its best light during the open house. Some listing agents like to use the "security and privacy" excuse to have visitors sign the visitor log they prepare, and others just ask visitors if they are under contract with a brokerage. If they're not, it's a good opportunity to ask them what they're looking for if your listing is not right for them so you can start sending and showing them other properties.

It's up to you whether you guide visitors through the property, but I find it's often best to ask them if they'd like to wander around or whether they'd like a guided tour. A no-pressure sales manner is the best way to approach visitors at your open house. Be available and helpful, but let visi-tors do their own thing if they prefer. Many people, whether they're alone or with someone else, like to simply walk around and view the property on their own, asking questions afterwards, if they have any. Make sure you follow up with anyone whose contact information you collected, whether realtor or buyer, after the open house.

Keeping the Seller Client Calm during the Sale Process

You'll probably know early on whether you're working with calm, trusting clients or nervous, controlling ones. Either way, remember that it is your job to sell their property at a price and on terms that they agree to. If you prepare the property and listing well and expose the property to the market appropriately, you should get interest that you can convert to an offer or offers. Clients who trust your knowledge and heed your advice will list the property at an appropriate price, and buyers' interest should be forthcom-ing. With more difficult clients, you might have no choice but to accept listing the property at a higher price or in a less than desirable condition, which means you should be prepared to educate and condition your clients that it may be necessary to lower the asking price or improve the appear-ance of the property after a few weeks if there has not been solid interest. The bottom line, which you may wish to share with your clients, is that all properties sell—it's just a question of at what price and on what terms.

Some pre-existing situations can make your clients more stressed during the selling process—for example, if they've already bought another house and have a closing date coming up. Their new mortgage may even be contingent on the equity they will get from the sale of their current house. In this case, don't feel it's imperative to sell their house and have it close before their new home does. It is important, however, to have a firm deal that they can use to obtain bridge financing, which will enable them to fulfill their obligation to close on their new property.

Most of the problems or issues that stress out sellers can be managed or avoided by good planning on your part. You need to educate clients about how much work they're going to have to put into the property before it goes on the market, the sacrifices they'll need to make from a lifestyle perspective for a week, or possibly several months (if the house is staged nicely, many of their personal effects will be going into storage, which makes cleaning, watching a DVD, using a desktop computer, and even having a varied wardrobe sometimes challenging), the fact that they'll have to leave the house for an hour or two at a time, perhaps quite often, to accommodate showings, and so on. If you understand the goals your clients hope to achieve by selling their property, you will be able to manage their potential stress. For example, if they are downsizing and money is not an issue, but they're going on a three-month vacation in a few weeks, then you need to sell fast so they can relax and enjoy their vacation. If your clients are selling due to a divorce and money is very tight, then you need to manage both of the desires they have: to sell quickly to get that phase of their lives behind them, and to maximize the selling price.

Dealing with Multiple Offers

Depending on the pricing strategy you employ when listing a property for sale, and the goals you and your clients have set, you can market a property by pricing it at, or a little above, the price you think it will sell for, and accept offers at any time, or you can attempt to attract a multiple-offer situation.

It is almost always better for a seller to have several offers to choose from, and sometimes even to be able to work the offers against each other to create a bidding-war scenario. However, I would rather have a sure thing 90 percent of the time than chase an extraordinary offer 10 percent of the time. I have, therefore, rarely listed a property with the express intent of promoting a bidding war.

A bidding war can be very lucrative for the seller, but it does carry risks. When a listing agent tells two or more buyers' agents that they should ask their clients to improve their offers, none of the buyers have any legal requirement to actually come back to the table, and the seller can be left without any offer to work with. Additionally, when price becomes the only focus (you can read in Chapter 15 that the price is just one element of a real estate deal, and that the terms and conditions can be just as, or far more, important), sellers are sometimes led to accept terms that don't necessarily align with their original goals.

The approach I prefer to take—though occasionally some situations will of course demand a different strategy—is to list a property at an asking price I can reasonably defend using data, facts, and logic, or to list slightly higher to allow for negotiations. If the property has been marketed to the target market appropriately, with all pertinent information made available to potential buyers and their realtors, then the property should sell for close to market value, at a minimum—and potentially for more than that, if several offers do come in.

Should you be in the (somewhat) enviable position of being a listing agent whose listing has attracted multiple offers (this could happen at a prescribed date and time, as you may have requested in your listing, or it could happen organically, where several offers come in within a few hours, or a day, of each other), then you need to strategically advise your client on how to proceed. As with many aspects of real estate brokerage, unless you have experience with, and are very comfortable in, a multiple-offer situation, you should ask for help or advice from a brokerage manager or an experienced colleague.

First, you'll need to read all of the offers thoroughly, noting the details, and you may find it helpful (both to you and to your client) to keep track of all the pertinent points so you can compare offers side by side. An Excel spreadsheet is useful for this, where you can set the first column as the buyer's name, then the rest as the price, closing date, irrevocable date and time, number of conditions, length of the conditions, type of conditions, and anything else that the seller should take into account, such as representations, warranties, inclusions, exclusions, chattels, fixtures, and so on. This should present a much clearer picture of how the offers stack up, and ensures that you won't miss a detail buried in an offer when you're presenting them to your client. Preparing such a spreadsheet, though, assumes that cooperating agents are not presenting the offers in person to your client. If that is the case, you can create a handwritten summary of each offer as it is presented, with a separate piece of paper for each offer (so the cooperating agents don't see your summary of other offers).

Eventually, a question that your client will have to ask himself, which you should be prepared to advise him on, is "Do I sign a specific offer back, or ask them all to present their best offer?" Each option has some risks. As I mention earlier in this section, asking all, or several, of the buyers to better their offers runs the risk that none will come back to you. Alternately, choosing one offer and trying to get a better deal for your client can result in the buyer not countering, which can leave you scrambling to salvage one of the earlier offers (and puts you and your client in a weaker position to negotiate). Something that many listing agents are starting to do in multiple-offer situations is simply to accept the strongest offer to avoid running the risk of having that buyer walk away if the listing agent tries to get her client a little more money.

If your client wants to sign only one offer back, how do you decide which one that is, and what do you communicate to agents with offers in the ring? This is where experience and a flair for business and negotiations come in handy. Again, better to swallow your pride and ask for assistance or guidance rather than go it on your own and potentially botch the deal, opening yourself up to liability and, of course, costing you a commission. Sellers naturally gravitate toward the highest price, and that is normal. However, make sure you compare the other terms. The closing date and the buyer's conditions are very important too. Does the closing date match with your client's preference? If he has already bought another house with a set closing date, can he afford to carry both properties for a period of time if the buyer with the preferred offer is asking for a long closing? As a seller, having no conditions in an offer is great, but make sure there is a decent deposit to discourage the buyer from trying to walk away from the deal. Some conditions are reasonable and should be expected. If all offers in a multiple-offer situation have financing and home-inspection conditions, you may have to live with them.

As the listing agent, you should make sure you discuss every offer with each buyer's agent. If an offer is unconditional, it can't hurt to ask the buyer's agent if her client is paying cash, or has financing otherwise arranged. Theoretically, your client can keep a deposit if the buyer of an unconditional deal walks away, but often those situations devolve into arguments and legal problems for everyone. It's much better to hear from a buyer's agent that her client thinks he'll get the necessary financing and advise your client of this, so your client can decide on whether to roll the dice and bet that the buyer will get appropriate financing, or to make the safe play and work with a more financially-grounded offer, or to simply accept a financing condition.

Property disclosure statements are called seller property information statements (SPISs) in Ontario, and it is very important that you understand them—both for your sake as well as the sake of your clients.

An SPIS is a document that sellers fill out, checking boxes and adding comments to questions such as:

- Does the subject property comply with the zoning?
- If not, is it legal non-conforming?
- What is under the carpeting?
- Is there any lead or galvanized plumbing on the property?

These questions, and the other 40-plus questions your clients have to consider in an SPIS, are not questions that every layperson or homeowner can easily answer. Often your clients rely on your guidance to fill out an SPIS.

There are a few questions you need to ask yourself with regard to an SPIS. First, should you even ask your clients to fill one out? Although you are not specifically required to have a seller fill out an SPIS due to regulatory codes of ethics, provincial legislation, and common law, there is an obligation of making full disclosure about a property. When it comes to using an SPIS to fulfill that obligation, you *should* ask a client to fill one out—but there is a difference between asking with the intent of getting it filled out, and asking just to cover all your bases from a regulatory perspective. If you have formally asked your seller to fill one out, you can legitimately claim to have made an appropriate effort at full disclosure about the property.

If you do a Google search for "SPIS," you will receive a plethora of results, many condemning the use of these forms. Since their introduction by the Ontario Real Estate Association (OREA) in 1993, there have been dozens of court cases in which the SPIS was the primary source of contention between the parties. The SPIS was originally created to protect sellers and realtors by allowing them to put in writing their knowledge of a property, so buyers could not complain after the fact that they were not aware of a deficiency with the property.

Real estate associations have been pushing their members to promote the use of this form, and many realtors do not understand the unintended consequences of doing so, making the SPIS a hot-button topic in real estate circles. Its few proponents feel that it can still protect sellers while informing buyers, but its many detractors feel that the exposure to liability and resulting litigation is simply too great for sellers and listing agents, and that real estate transactions can be completed more safely and quickly without an SPIS.

The pros of having an SPIS include the fact that a seller is able to declare knowledge of a problem or defect with a property in order to be open and transparent and thus avoid potential litigation down the road from a buyer who claims she was kept in the dark. However, once an SPIS is filled out (and there is a field on MLS listings for the listing agent to indicate whether an SPIS is available from the seller), there is an expectation that the seller has shared his full knowledge of his property, not just the more important potential issues. Realtors place themselves at risk when sellers ask them for advice or guidance in filling out the form, because the seller may not know exact details about his own property—in other words, the existence of a problem or potential problem. As soon as this assistance is provided, the realtor is more likely to be found liable and accountable by a court of law for the contents of the SPIS. Furthermore, a realtor who does not use her best attempts to know the property intimately and address any contradictions in the SPIS with the seller is again liable for misrepresentation.

Consult both your broker of record and manager about using an SPIS in general, and potentially on a case-by-case basis, to make sure you are properly advised and protected.

•　•　•

You have held a successful open house for your client, received offers, and reviewed them carefully with your client. Now you need to guide your client through the process of accepting an offer (or rejecting it) and sorting out the terms of an offer so the deal can close. Chapter 9 reviews various scenarios that an offer might take, and what you need to change in an offer before sending it back to the buyer's agent. Once you have negotiated a firm deal, there are still many ways you can help your client that differentiate your level of service from that of other agents.

Getting to Closing

The title of this chapter is intentionally somewhat misleading. To start, I explain how a deal can be accepted. It is not always the seller who accepts an offer. In fact, I think that sellers and buyers split the honour of which party is the one to accept an offer. Sometimes, especially today in certain Canadian cities that are hot seller's markets, there is so much pressure on buyers to make their initial offer an excellent one so that sellers may accept offers when they are received. To do this, if standard real estate forms are being used for the offer, the seller signs and dates the appropriate area of the signature page to show that he or she is in agreement with the entire offer document, and also signs a section typically called "Confirmation of Acceptance." Lastly, most real estate agreements to sell or lease property also have a section called "Acknowledgement," which the seller signs, indicating that he has received a fully executed copy of the agreement.

If the deal you're working on is a traditional situation, the buyer makes your client an offer, and when you review it with your client, most of the time she does not agree with the offered price or the terms. At that point, I suggest that you ask your client how she feels about the offer, which points she feels she couldn't live with, and which she'd rather not accept, but would if she had to, in order to eventually make a deal. You should now know your client well enough to ask if you could offer her your professional opinion. Taking into account what she has told you, let her know how hard you feel you can push, and on which points (price, closing date, chattels, conditions, and so on), and, if you have some concrete reasons, relay why you feel those are good points to negotiate. Your reasons could be based on market and neighbourhood information, details you gleaned from speaking with the buyer's agent, or simply good business and negotiation skills you possess.

You now know that the seller would like to respond to this offer, but does not agree with the terms. The next step is for you to cross out anything you'd like to change in the offer and, if it is to be replaced with something rather than merely deleted, write, as close as possible to what you are replacing, the wording of the point your client wants to insert. You can be crossing out a price or deposit amount and replacing it with a different one (you need to cross out both the numeric and alphanumeric sections and replace both); taking out or adding chattels or fixtures; changing the closing date; or modifying, deleting, or adding a condition, clause, or attachment (usually labelled "Schedule A," "Schedule B," and so on).

Negotiating a Deal

Here is an example of how a typical deal could be negotiated and which party does what:

1. The buyer makes an offer; his agent has signed the cooperating brokerage's commission-trust section of the offer.

2. The seller doesn't agree with everything in the offer, but based on her agent's advice, she feels there is hope of arriving at an agreement with the buyer if he signs it back. The seller changes the price and the closing date, deletes a chandelier that the buyer had included as part of the purchase, deletes the buyer's condition to sell his house before this deal firms up, and adds her own condition to have the agreement reviewed and approved by her lawyer.

3. The buyer is happy to have received a response from the seller and accepts all the changes, but cannot accept the price. The buyer lowers the price to a level he can live with, but that is higher than his original offer.

4. The seller receives the offer back from the buyer and is happy to see that all her changes were accepted, but she is still not getting the price she would like. After speaking with her realtor, the seller accepts the offer in its entirety, having decided that she doesn't want to risk losing this buyer by trying to get a few thousand more dollars into the price—especially because all the other points are what she wanted, including the closing date, and the fact that she has a condition to have her lawyer review the document.

Below, I list the most common scenarios in which the seller receives an offer and, depending on what she accepts (or doesn't) in the offer, what you, as the listing agent, need to change before sending it back to the buyer's agent.

- **Scenario 1:** The seller does not like the offer at all and does not believe a deal will result from it. You respond to the buyer's realtor by telling him that:

  - You appreciate his client's offer, but the seller feels that they are too far apart on too many points to arrive at an agreement.

  - If his client would consider making a more attractive offer, you'd be happy to present it to the seller.

- **Scenario 2:** The seller does not agree with most of the points in the offer, but decides to respond by:

  - Changing the price

  - Changing the closing date

  - Changing the irrevocable from buyer to seller, and the date and time

  - Changing any chattel or fixture that the seller does, or does not, want to be part of the offer

  - Changing, deleting, or amending any condition or clause as necessary

  - Adding any condition or clause as necessary

  - Having the seller initial the bottom of each page

  - Having the seller sign and date the signature page

- **Scenario 3:** The seller agrees with most of the points in the offer and decides to respond by:

  - Changing just the points in the offer that the seller cannot live with

  - Adding any conditions or clauses as necessary

  - Having the seller initial the bottom of each page

  - Having the seller sign and date the signature page

There are two terms in the offering process that you need to understand perfectly, because you will need to explain them to your clients:

- An accepted offer is simply where one party (buyer or seller, it doesn't matter which), agrees to the offer from the other party as is, and does not make any changes to it.

- A conditional offer is most often an offer that has been accepted but with one or more conditions. Once those conditions are waived or satisfied, that offer becomes firm, which is synonymous with unconditional. An accepted offer can also be a firm offer right away, but only if there are no conditions.

What this means is that neither party can back out of the deal without consequences, because they have both agreed to close the transaction on the agreed-upon date, for the agreed-upon price, and on the agreed-upon terms. If the buyer refuses to close as outlined in the offer, then he risks losing his deposit (which is one reason for a listing agent and seller to insist on as large a deposit as possible, because facing the prospect of losing it is sometimes sufficient incentive for a buyer to stay with the deal he struck with the seller), and further risks litigation from the seller. If the seller refuses to close, the deposit should be returned to the buyer, but often is held in trust pending the outcome of the litigation that may ensue. If the seller refuses to close, most listing agreements state that the commission the seller agreed to pay the listing brokerage is due and payable by the seller to the listing brokerage, because it has fulfilled its obligation to find and negotiate an offer that became firm, but it will not close due to the seller.

Helping the Client beyond the Deal

Once a deal goes firm, most of the pressure is off of you, the listing agent, because you've done everything you promised to do for the seller. This is, however, the point at which the difference between average and great realtors becomes apparent. An average realtor will move on to the next deal. A great realtor will find the time to answer the seller's questions, send her reminders of things she needs to do before closing, and stay in regular contact so that the seller does not feel like a mere business transaction, but rather a valued client. I find that for every one negative thing people remember, you need to do at least 10 good things to counter that negative one. Keeping this in mind, even if you were a superstar realtor during the pre-listing, pre-marketing, listing, and marketing periods; the negotiations; and the conditional periods, if you disappear as soon as the deal goes firm, and your client doesn't really hear from you again, or not very often, that is what she is going to remember the most—that as soon as the deal was as good as done, you were nowhere to be seen or heard.

Some of the ways in which you can be useful and of service to your clients once a deal becomes firm are:

- Ensure that arrangements have been made for wherever they are moving to next. Hopefully you represented them in buying their next property, but if you didn't, show that you are thinking about that move.

- Send them a reminder to arrange for all their utilities, including telephone, cable, Internet, hydro, gas, and so on, to be disconnected from their present house and new accounts set up for their next property.

- Remind them to make an appointment with their lawyer to understand the steps they need to take leading up to closing the transaction.

- If they have children, send them useful information (even if you have done so previously) such as the locations of parks, schools, libraries, community centres, and so on, in the area they're moving to.

- Ask them to consider referring family, friends, and co-workers to you.

- Remind them to arrange for professional movers, moving supplies, or a moving van or truck.

- Send them a list of the items they have included in the sale of their property, so they don't forget and take them when they move.

- Call your clients every few weeks to make sure they are comfortable with the upcoming closing and ask if they have any questions.

● ● ●

Many realtors may feel that once they have an offer on their listing, they are almost done doing the deal. I disagree. You are really less than halfway to finishing the sale. Not only does the offer need to be negotiated, but also it is your duty, when representing a seller, to advise her whether she is actually getting what she can or should for her property. Sometimes listing agents don't fight hard enough to get their clients the highest offer they can, simply because they don't want to, don't feel like they have to, or think that pushing the envelope will jeopardize a potential deal.

At one time, agents who controlled listings made the most money. Things have changed in the last few years, and some agents who work with buyers more often do extremely well. In Part III of this book, I teach you how to represent buyers, help them figure out what they really want and need, show them how to find the right properties, and, finally, negotiate their lease or purchase.

Representing the Buyer

10

Knowing What Your Buyer Client *Really* Wants

It is your job—first and foremost—to represent your clients' interests in any situation. Representing a buyer and his or her interests is very different from representing a seller.

One of the first things to remember, especially in the context of negotiating with listing agents, is that your client rarely has to buy a specific property. A seller has to sell his property, so he may be in a more vulnerable position compared to that of a buyer. This means that you, as the agent, should coach your buyer from the first day of your relationship or property search to not become emotionally attached to any specific property. This is much easier said than done, as most buyers think they are in complete control when they start their real estate search, but they can easily fall in love with a property or, after a long and emotionally trying search over a number of months, they may become desperate and say, "That's the one." The problem is, as soon as buyers allow their emotions to get too high, they inevitably settle for inferior properties or spend more money than they had intended to. Your job, as their agent, is to prevent buyers, as much as possible, from reaching such an unfortunate outcome.

It is, therefore, very important to guide your buyers right from the outset, especially if it is their first property purchase. As I discuss in Chapter 1, each realtor, consciously or not, develops her own style and approach when working with clients. My own approach with buyers is typically as follows, although various situations do require me to deviate from this path from time to time.

Meeting Face to Face

I always meet with a potential buyer client. At the beginning of my real estate career, I did not truly understand the importance of meeting the buyer, and sometimes started work on finding a property for a buyer when I had only been contacted by him via phone or email. Often, when you are starting out, or going through a dry spell, it is so exciting to have someone say he would like you to act as his realtor that you forget to be cautious with your time and advice.

When I finally understood that it was incredibly unlikely (read: just about impossible) for me to do a deal without meeting a buyer right at the beginning of the relationship, I made the initial meeting my first step when representing a buyer. This sounds simple enough, but many people call you about an ad or a listing, or on the advice of a friend, and have what seems to be a very casual question about real estate. You answer the query, then a week or two later, there is another question. Before you know it, you've spent hours, or days, working for someone you've never met, and you're well on your way to not closing a deal with her.

If someone contacts me, or vice versa, in person or by phone or email, I always say we should sit down for 15 minutes to chat. You can handle this however you like. You can suggest meeting over coffee to put each other's faces to names or you can say, as I do most of the time, that you need to meet because you have questions that you need to ask before you can start looking for a property. However you go about it, make a face-to-face appointment. The exception is if he is an out-of-town client who will only be visiting when you have properties to show. In that case, you have to decide whether it is worth doing a little bit of work before being able to meet him on his first visit—but be aware that it's likely he will also be meeting other realtors on that same visit.

Whether I already know my potential buyer or not, I want her to feel comfortable when we meet to discuss real estate for the first time. I sometimes ask where she would like to meet or, if I think I know her well enough, I suggest meeting at her house (this allows you to get to know her and even get her to take you around her home and point out things she likes and doesn't like, so you know what to look for or avoid in your search). You can also suggest meeting at the buyer's workplace, in a public place such as a coffee shop, or at your brokerage offices.

Be sure to confirm an appointment by email. If the appointment is a few days away, call or email a reminder (often my assistant does this for me). I feel it is quite important to arrive a little early for that first meeting. If you're in a city with a lot of traffic (I'm sure my Toronto compatriots understand exactly why I feel it necessary to mention this), make certain that you're giving yourself a lot of margin time. It's better to be half an hour early and have to wait for your client, than to be five minutes late. This is because you are still in the "making a good first impression" phase, and this is the time that is crucial to building a solid relationship.

You should dress how you feel is appropriate. I am a casual, or business-casual, dresser, as that fits well with my business style, but you may prefer to always wear a suit, a skirt, or even jeans. In my opinion, your presentation is more important than your clothing. Make sure that you are clean, are well-kept, make eye contact, shake hands with your potential buyer firmly, open doors for your clients, say "please" and "thank you," and so on.

When you sit down with your client for the first time, you have to feel your way through the conversation. Given my very casual business style, I usually begin to talk about light subjects or ask a few personal questions, such as: Do you work near here? What do you do? Do you have any kids? How old are they, and what are their names? Are you moving for a specific reason or for several reasons?

For most people, when they are talking about themselves, they feel more comfortable, and they relate that feeling of comfort to you. Having someone feel comfortable with you is essential to a successful relationship.

Questions to Ask the Client

Once you are past the general niceties, you can start asking questions related to your client's search. I normally do this before discussing the process or having the buyer commit to using me as his realtor. Once again, if you can get the client talking about what he wants in his future property, psychologically he is already working with you. For each property and buyer, you need to ask various questions. Here are some you may want to consider asking:

- What is your price range (or your maximum price)?

- Are there specific areas that you are interested in?

- Are you in the market for a condo, or a semi-detached or detached house? (For commercial, choices would be retail, office, industrial, and so on.)

- How much money can you put as a down payment?

- Have you been pre-qualified for a new mortgage?

- If you currently own your home, will you need to sell it, or will you keep it as an investment that you'll rent out? Do you prefer to sell your home first, or after you purchase your new one? Depending on your specific circumstances, would you like to hear the pros and cons of selling your home before buying, or buying your next home before you sell?

- How many bedrooms and bathrooms are absolutely necessary, and how many would you like if possible within your price range?

- Are you looking for an average house with average finishes, with some room for improvement, or would you like something completely renovated with modern finishes, or, lastly, would you like a property into which you can really pour some time and money, either to increase the value or to be able to be in control of what your home will look and feel like? Are there any upcoming life changes you should consider now, which may change the type or size of property you'll need, such as retirement, a new child, or children or other family moving out of your house?

- Have you been looking at some properties yet? Online? Open houses?

One of the approaches I sometimes use, especially if I feel that the buyer is likely to be hard to please, is to draw two columns on a blank piece of paper and title one column "Needs" and the other column "Wants"— and I make sure the buyer can see me as I do this exercise. Then I tell her I'm going to ask her some questions (from the list above), and that I'd like her to try to answer each for the "Needs" and "Wants" column. For example, "How many washrooms do you need and how many do you want (or, would it be nice to have?)" and "You may like to have parking for three cars, but could you make do with just two (you have two cars after all, not three)?" Asking questions in this fashion allows you to determine what, in your client's mind, is the minimum that is acceptable, and what she would like to get, if possible. The property she ends up buying or leasing is likely to have a mixture of both needs and wants.

Use the Funnel Approach

If your meeting is going well and your client is talking freely about what he'd like in his future property, I find it easiest when talking about location to simply ask for the north, south, east, and west boundaries, and, depending on how large an area it represents, any pockets that he would like to avoid. For example:

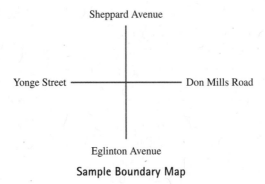

Sample Boundary Map

Another point I cover with new buyers is that I use a funnel approach. I explain to them (or sometimes draw it on a piece of paper) that I start the property search with broad criteria, and, as they give me feedback on properties I send or show them, I continue to narrow the search criteria, so that eventually each property I send them is a very likely candidate for them to purchase.

Be prepared to help your clients answer your questions about what they want and need. Some people simply don't know, while others are indecisive, and still others think they know exactly what they want, but they're wrong—usually because they don't realize that what they want is not realistic with the budget they have to work with. If your clients don't know whether they'd prefer a semi-detached house or a detached one, explain the pros and cons of each option to them. If they don't know how many bedrooms they need, ask about their current living arrangement, and what the near- to mid-future holds for them. For example, do they often have guests over who spend the night? Do they have in-laws or other family who visit for a few days at a time? Do they have children now, and do they expect any more? Not only do realtors have access to properties for sale and lease, we also do the majority of document preparation and deal negotiation, and we must act as guides to our clients. If you want to be a good and ethical realtor who is successful in the long term, you must not focus on your commission to the extent that you are giving advice to your clients that is not in their best interest. This is one of the toughest points for new (and, unfortunately, many senior) realtors to accept and embrace. My philosophy is to serve the clients I choose to work with honestly and to the best of my ability. If this means I make slightly less on a deal or I suggest clients should wait a little while before buying, selling, or leasing a property, I more than make up for a smaller or deferred commission with the amount of repeat business and referrals I garner from those same clients. Real estate brokerage work is never a get-rich-quick game, but if you plant the right seeds the appropriate way, they mature very nicely, often at a varied pace, which gives you a steady income stream, instead of one with peaks and valleys.

Make it clear to your client how you will communicate with her going forward—will you email her regularly or only when there is a property of interest?—and ensure she understands the following two crucial points:

- She must give you feedback on the properties you send her. This is the only way you will know whether you are on the right track, and how you will keep a finger on the pulse of your client's needs and wants. These will evolve as she sees properties both on paper and in person. If you're not in tune with these changes, you won't be sending her the right properties, and her trust in your abilities to find her a property will steadily diminish until she decides to work with someone else.

- Depending on her time frame to buy or lease, if she is serious about finding a property, she has to act quickly if she sees something she likes. While market conditions are constantly changing (sometimes buyers are at the controls in a deal, and at other times sellers are), one thing is always true: you never know when another buyer or tenant is going to come along and either scoop a deal away from you or become the competition, which is going to drive the price of a property up for your client.

Your first meeting with a buyer may or may not be a good time to bring up questions on cash and financing, but I normally do try to touch on these topics. As mentioned earlier in this chapter, you should ask whether your client has arranged for financing (if she requires financing). For most buyers, this means being pre-qualified for a new mortgage, and making sure that they have a clear and realistic picture—ideally from their bank or a mortgage broker—of what they can afford and where their down payment, closing costs, and buffer money (the term "buffer money" is one I use to cover any unplanned eventualities, such as temporary unemployment, an injury that results in no income for a period of time, or a major home component, such as a furnace or roof needing to be replaced urgently) are going to come from—for example, RRSPs for first-time buyers, savings, or monetary gifts from family or friends.

TECHNOLOGY HELPERS: A DAILY MLS FEED

Most Canadian real estate boards allow their members to program a set of criteria for a specific client, and have servers that email, on a daily basis, any new MLS listing that has come on the market for sale or lease that matches the programmed criteria.

The funny thing is, the Toronto Real Estate Board sends out these automatic emails for programmed prospects between 3:00 a.m. and 5:00 a.m. every day. I cannot count how many clients have congratulated me on working very hard for them, very early, every day. I usually explain how the system works to most of them, but I have to admit, every now and then, I just nod with a serious look on my face, and say, "Anything for my clients!"

When you sit down to program a search (or "Prospect," as it's called on the TREB's MLS) you're going to take all of the criteria you got from your buyer clients when you met with them, and input the information so they automatically receive MLS listings that match their needs. Do this for as many clients and potential clients as you can, because it is one of the easiest ways to keep your name in front of them, and they often don't realize that it's zero effort for you once you've programmed their criteria as a prospect. Sometimes a seller might ask to be kept abreast of what is happening in his neighbourhood, and this is another great example of when you should program an automatic search-and-email.

The only decision you really need to make is whether to have all of the results automatically emailed to your client daily, or whether you'd like them sent to you, at which point you'd review the matching MLS listings one by one, sending only the ones you select to your client. This allows you to filter out those listings that might have something unappealing to your clients, and helps you to appear to be a much more on-the-ball realtor to your clients. Of course, this takes a lot of your time. I like to tell my clients that I can work only within the parameters of my real estate board's MLS search parameters, which are not very flexible, so they will sometimes receive listings that don't exactly match their criteria, and they should ignore those. The flip side of this is that your clients sometimes receive listings that you would have culled, but they might actually consider buying.

MLS search on your website
You've probably noticed that many agents now provide a search for available MLS listings on their websites. The MLS listing feed is known in the industry

(*continued*)

as an Internet data exchange (IDX) feed. IDX feeds are raw data feeds sent out by local real estate boards. These feeds are typically provided by third-party web hosting companies that specialize in websites for real estate agents. However, IDX feeds can, theoretically, be hosted by any web host for a bona fide real estate agent. The main advantage of using a specialist is the ease and speed in which you can deploy IDX on your website. To use a raw IDX feed, formatting of the data is required as well as adhering to a number of MLS conditions. The web specialist companies tend to streamline the requirements and pre-format the feed data to a useable format. Some providers, such as RealWeb, based in Toronto, integrate customer-relations-management functions (like the well-known CRM Salesforce) with the MLS feed and fill-in forms. A sign-in form that captures name, address, email, phone number, and the desired parameters of a property search takes that information and adds it directly into the CRM portion of the system as a potential lead. The agent can then follow up with the lead, and set up automatic mailings of MLS listings based on the parameters captured on sign-up.

Real estate web-hosting companies often combine an IDX feed with other services that enhance the MLS search process. Integrating Google Maps to pinpoint the location of properties is frequently added, as well as neighbourhood rating services such as WalkScore to help gauge the convenience of an area.

Taking the Emotion Out of Buying a Property

We should all be in this business to complete transactions that result in satisfied clients, who are likely to use our services again and refer us to other consumers. To help you arrive at this mutually beneficial end result, I talk in Chapter 4 about managing your clients' expectations and getting a good feel for their goals early on in the relationship. If you've gotten a good handle on their needs and wants and you've gotten their feedback on properties for sale that you've shown them on paper or in person, then you should be ready to let them know when a property meets their needs (and hopefully includes a few of their wants as well) and they should seriously consider presenting an offer.

Of course, before rushing into preparing an offer, you should be able to advise your buyers about the value that that property represents. Make sure you find comparables and explain them to your clients. This is the best way to understand whether you are going to be preparing an offer in the attempt to get the property for a good deal, or whether your clients will be paying market value, or above—which is not always bad, but your buyers need to know that this is the case so they can make an educated decision.

Helping your clients work through and survive the range of emotions they will experience when buying a property takes patience and understanding from you, as well as an ability to put them and their interests before your own and your commission. The only times you should seriously consider putting your commission first are:

- When you're asked to work on a small deal (every realtor's opinion of what a small deal is varies). I often tell potential clients that I cannot commit to doing very much work if the deal is small, but I give them tips on what they can do themselves and let them know that I'm always available to answer questions.

- If the seller, landlord, or listing agent will not pay your commission. In this case, you need to ask your buyer or tenant to budget to pay your commission.

- If the seller, landlord, or listing agent is offering a small commission for the size of the deal, or the amount of work you will be required to put in. I normally go back to the seller, landlord, or listing agent and tell him that I can only work on the deal if I'm compensated appropriately.

The best way to understand the emotions your clients are feeling when they are buying a property is for you to communicate with them and understand their goals and fears. For example, if money is an issue and they are stretching their budget because they have not found anything, despite a long search, in their initial price range, then you might need to remind them that there is no rush, and that they should give you a little more time to expose them to moderately priced properties for a while longer. If, however, they are first-time homebuyers, and are getting cold feet or are nervous about carrying a reasonable mortgage, perhaps you should remind them of the practical and financial differences there are between owning and leasing, and find a way to calm their fears with facts and numbers.

There are only a few very common scenarios in which you see clients become emotional. I go through them one by one, and show you how you can help:

- Your buyers have been searching for a long time and have not found anything they like.

If it is appropriate to the circumstances, you should suggest that they look in a different area or broaden their search area, increase the price range they have been sticking to, or simply lower their standards if they cannot spend more money. This can all be done with tact and an empathetic ear.

- They have made several offers on properties, all of which have been rejected, or they lost out in bidding wars.

  Depending on what you feel the buyers' state of mind is, you should either counsel patience and ensure that they are familiar with all the aggressive buying preparatory tactics available (mortgage pre-approval, pre-inspections, having sold their previous house already, and so on) so that they are able to present very aggressive offers, or suggest that they take a mini-break from the property search, so that they can find their emotional balance to avoid making any large purchasing decisions that they might regret down the road.

- Your clients love a property, but cannot afford it.

  In this case, you should advise them that it's your job to make sure that they remember the property-buying goals they set out with, one of which has to do with price. You can point out some of the elements that they liked about this property, and let them know that some, or many, of them should be found in properties within their financial reach.

- Your buyers have made an offer or received a signed-back offer from the sellers and are prepared to accept what they wouldn't have originally because they are so emotionally invested in the property that they cannot bear the thought of losing the deal.

  You have to tread lightly here and, eventually, do whatever your clients want. But if you feel there is room to protect them or their money, you should advise them of how you feel. They'll make the final decision, but they should know that a real estate professional is suggesting a little more patience or taking a small risk for a potentially good reward.

This is a good place to talk about the emotions that realtors erroneously bring to the table. As I mention briefly at the beginning of this chapter, you should almost always place your clients' needs ahead of your commission. This is anathema to many realtors, but this is because they are short-sighted and have not experienced, or don't understand, the power of telling a client not to buy now or to spend less, when it is understood that this advice is going to result in a lower commission for the agent. Such selfless behaviour almost always does wonders for the level of confidence and trust your clients have in you, and often makes them more loyal to you than before, making them more likely to refer you to others who may need your services.

I can understand very well what it is like to be a realtor who needs that next commission to happen just to hold things together (I've been there!). However, you are often shooting yourself in the foot if you get that one deal done by being less than honest with your clients, or by pushing them to buy something they should not have, or pay more than they should have, because they'll probably figure it out eventually (remember, real estate is one of those topics that Canadians talk about a lot, and one's personal experiences often get mentioned), and never use you again or refer you to anyone. Even worse, if you've annoyed the wrong person, he'll find out how to file an official complaint against you with your brokerage, real estate board, and regulatory associations. You won't last long as a licensed agent if you get too many of those.

Just to illustrate how powerful this positive attitude of great service and honesty can be, let me leave you with my experience. Several times I have been representing buyers whom I advised to wait to buy, pay less, or buy a smaller property. Out of gratitude, they referred one or more new clients to me, with whom I did deals before I closed one with my initial clients.

• • •

Although helping your client understand what she wants and needs in a property so you can assist her properly and efficiently (time is, after all, money for salespeople) is important in the buying process, much of this will become clear once you start showing your client properties. As I explain in Chapter 11, this real-time observation of your buyers' reactions to location, property features and finishes, and what they can get for the money they have to spend, is essential to moulding your property search for your clients. Keep in mind that most people plan to finance their real estate purchase, and reminding them to get pre-approved can help everyone involved save time and money, and ensure they don't miss their ideal property.

11

Showing Properties to Your Clients

The most common way for a buyer who is working with a realtor to see a property is for the realtor to schedule an appointment to show a property that is listed for sale (or lease) to his buyer.

If you have been diligent and honest with yourself in selecting your buyer clients, showing them properties is quite easy to do and one of the most important steps in the buying process. You research properties for the buyer to see and then schedule appointments to show those properties. It is always ideal to have a buyer representation agreement (BRA) signed (as I discuss in Part II) and currently in force with your clients, so if they are exposed to other realtors, your commission is protected.

There are many realtors who want to accompany their clients to every open house they attend. These same realtors also designate listings from the MLS for their buyer clients to review. This practice is restrictive and not recommended. I disagree with both of these practices because the more properties my clients are exposed to, the faster they get a solid idea of what they want and like. I normally ask them to let the listing agent at an open house know they are working with a realtor. I do this out of respect for the listing agent, so he does not assume he'll be able to double-end the deal, but also to remind my clients that I am there to represent and advise them. I encourage my clients to go online, preferably on www.realtor.ca (the new www.mls.ca) for residential properties and www.icx.ca for commercial properties. These public sites allow non-realtors to view all properties currently listed on the MLS in Canada. The more time my clients spend browsing properties on these sites, the more excited and involved they become in the process of finding their next property, and the sooner they are able to eliminate properties with features they don't like, properties they can't afford, or properties located in areas they don't ultimately like.

Realtors should be reassured that even though their clients are looking at other realtors' listings online, the public can only see a certain amount of the information regarding listed properties on these sites. New listings are delayed by one day, which means that agents see new properties sooner with our access to MLS—and our clients will receive any new properties that match the criteria we have programmed into automatic searches (called "prospects" on Toronto MLS), before they would see them on realtor.ca or icx.ca.

This is also a good test of your relationship with your clients. If they are scanning properties online, and they intend to work with you, you can be sure they will email or call you with questions about specific properties that have caught their eyes, and even ask you to arrange to show them certain ones.

Don't get the wrong idea—I still go to open houses with my clients. However, I think it is a healthy part of the process for my clients to casually visit a few open houses on a Saturday or Sunday morning, if that is what they like to do. When I do accompany my clients, I have found it best to keep an open mind concerning listing agents' different styles, and even prepare my clients for the various welcomes we can expect. Some agents throw open the front door and welcome everyone casually, whether the clients have a realtor accompanying them or not. Others tightly control access to the property and lock the front door as they show a potential buyer, with or without his realtor, through the house. Still others put on a lavish spread of coffee, tea, sparkling water, pop, sweets, vegetables with dip, and some finger foods; have music playing throughout the home; and have an official guest list to register in.

Preparing to Show Properties

Now, on to the most common scenario: You are going to make an appointment to show a property to your clients. Your clients have either asked to see a property, or have agreed to see one you have suggested to them. How you proceed depends on how well you know your clients, how long you have been searching for a property together, how well they know what they want, and whether they are truly ready to buy.

The following is for an average property in an average situation. If you're going to show a hot property that is likely to be in high demand, you should do more research ahead of time, find good comparables, and perhaps draft a simple offer, just in case your clients feel the need to present an offer on the spot. In most other situations, you should print out a copy of the MLS listing in client-full mode (for your client), and a copy in broker-full mode (for your reference at the showing). Make sure to print out any

MLS attachments, as well as any other useful information, depending on what you feel your clients will want to know, such as local school information, neighbourhood specifics, comparable sales or rentals (as applicable), and any details the listing agent sent you.

You should now call the listing brokerage and request a showing for a specific day and time. I normally ask for a full hour for the showing (for example, a showing from 1 p.m. to 2 p.m. tomorrow), and request that the listing agent does not book other showings during that same time. It is extremely annoying and potentially very awkward to have another realtor show up with her clients to show them through the property while you're trying to do the same—although I understand what an agent is trying to achieve when they do this. I rarely get angry in front of clients, but this is one situation that does infuriate me: when I arrive with my clients to show a property and we are just behind another realtor and her clients. In one particular case, the agent got the keys out of the lock box, opened the front door for her clients, then turned to me and said, "I guess they have double-booked us. I'll show first, then you can." She then proceeded to lock the door in my face.

The next step is to wait for the listing brokerage to send a showing confirmation to your brokerage. Depending on how you are set up, your brokerage will then forward you a showing confirmation with showing instructions. This is now most often done via email. If you do not receive a confirmation within an hour or so of speaking with the listing broker-age, I suggest you call them back and ask whether they have been able to do so yet. There are thousands of showings every day of properties listing on, for example, the TREB MLS, and mistakes are made. Other reasons you may not yet have heard include: the property is no longer available (sold, conditional or firm; or taken off the market); the listing agent has requested that he approves each showing request (this is often done so that the listing agent can be present at the showing, or because he wants to make sure he has the buyer's realtor's contact information in order to speak with her or send her information about the property before the showing); the office staff at the listing brokerage are too busy; your bro-kerage's office staff have not gotten around to sending you the showing confirmation, or are too busy; or your request simply fell through the cracks somewhere.

Typically, once I have received confirmation of the showing date and time, I print out a broker-full and a client-full version of the MLS listing (assuming the property in question is listing on MLS), as well as any attach-ments such as floor plans or property inspection summaries, and any fea-ture sheet or property package. Then I write the date, time, duration, and lock box code and location (if applicable), at the bottom of the broker-full version of the listing. The client-full version, as well as the copy of all the attachments you have printed, is for your clients, should they like to refer to them during the showing, and you retain your own copies for reference. Your clients will invariably ask you many questions; the papers you have proactively printed out can help you answer questions such as the following: Does this house have air conditioning? How many square feet is the house? How deep is the lot?

Whether you meet your clients at each property—you drive your car and they drive there in their own, or you meet at one location and go to the subsequent showings together in one car—is a choice based on the type of realtor you are, similar to whether you wear a suit and tie or dress more casually when meeting with clients. Keep in mind that if you do drive your clients around in your car, you are likely assuming some sort of liability for them, and you should check with your insurance company to see if you are covered in case something happens while you are driving your clients.

There are pros and cons to driving together and separately. If you have a good relationship with your clients, driving together allows you to discuss the property you just viewed, and the next one on the list, as well as the neighbourhood you are driving through. These can be invaluable pieces of information as you are continuously learning what your clients like and want. Similarly, if you don't know your clients very well, spending time in a car with them usually allows you to get to know them better. However, sometimes clients want to be able to discuss properties privately, or they (or you) may not have a very sociable personality, which may make the car ride uncomfortable.

If you are showing more than one property to your clients, try to arrive at the first appointment on time. Then, if you have properly staggered your viewing appointments (for example, depending on how far each one is from the others, two showings from 12:00 p.m. to 1:00 p.m., two more from 12:30 p.m. to 1:30 p.m., and one from 1:30 p.m. to 2:30 p.m.), you have the ultimate flexibility in being able to go through showings quickly if it is evident those properties are not good candidates for your clients, or to allow your clients to linger if they really like certain ones.

Negotiating Lock Boxes and Showing Etiquette

The majority of MLS-listed commercial and residential properties for lease and sale in Ontario have lock boxes set up by the listing agents to allow for quick and easy showings (however, it is more common in commercial for the listing agent to be present at showings, either because it is his or his client's preference). I found it interesting that the times I brokered deals in Quebec (for example, a client, whose house I sold in Toronto when she decided to move to Montreal, insisted that I help her find and negotiate the purchase of her new home in that city), there were no lock boxes. It seems to come from a combination of a fear of liability as well as the evolution of real estate culture in Quebec, because realtors with buyers book showings and meet the listing agent at the property each and every time. I argued with some listing agents that it made my job difficult, because I could not predict how much traffic there would be between showings, and my clients would not have the option of spending more time at properties of particular interest. The response from the agents was, invariably, that this was the way it was done in Montreal.

I am still undecided whether the "lock box" or "listing agent present for showing" method is better, because although I find the lack of a lock box inconvenient, a real estate deal seems much more likely to happen in Montreal (that is, a buyer purchases after seeing fewer properties, and a seller is able to sell with few showings) because the listing agent or a (hopefully) knowledgeable and informed colleague is always present to answer questions. This is more important than it may seem at first glance. Buyers often ask a lot of questions at a showing, and because it is not their real-tor's listing, it can be difficult for the realtor to answer all of the questions in an accurate and timely fashion. This means that buyers may pass on a property that might have fit the bill, because they either don't have the cor-rect information or have lost interest by the time the information is made available to them. Another reason for having the listing agent present for showings is that real estate brokerage is hugely affected by relationships and interactions between people. I often say that if the two realtors involved in a transaction have a good rapport from the beginning, the deal is half done. So, when realtors meet face to face, it is an opportunity for them to allow genuine human warmth to come to the forefront and for them to make a good initial impression on each other.

If the property you are showing does have a lock box, make sure that you have the code to open it, as well as its location, before you arrive. For freehold properties, the lock box is typically affixed to the front door, a rail-ing, or a hydro or utility box or pipe. In condo buildings, a lock box can be found either on hydro or utility boxes or pipes in the nearest stairwell on the same floor as the unit in question, or even a board of plywood with cables to attach each lock box. Alternatively, you will sometimes have to show identification and a business card to the concierge or security desk before they will release the key for the unit to you.

A well-thought-out lock box area in a condo building.

Here's a little trick that some realtors have started to adopt, and that I find very helpful for the realtors and the clients involved. When you place a lock box on a property (specific to condos where there can be many lock boxes in the same area) clearly mark your lock box with a coloured ribbon, your business card on the back, or both, to help the showing agent find yours quickly, and include this information in the showing instructions. It sucks to try the same code on 20 boxes when your client is waiting—especially in the pouring rain! This is especially helpful and important in condo buildings where there are many units for sale, where there are not a good variety of different locations to affix a lock box, or where the building management has designated an area specifically for lock boxes. See the above picture of an excellent lock box area that a Toronto condo placed in its lobby, around the corner from the front/security desk. What a relief for realtors who can just go straight to the box number that the listing brokerage gave them, and enter the code to open it, instead of navigating concrete stairwells or underground parking garages, where they are often found, and negotiating dozens of similar-looking boxes.

When you do have the key in hand, make sure that you knock on the entrance door. If you show enough properties, you invariably arrive at one that the listing agent has assured you will be empty, but where you find the seller or tenant still there. This is not normally a problem as the seller (or tenant) usually allows you and your clients in, or asks you to wait a minute while he gathers his things and leaves to give you privacy.

However, I know that the young lady who once answered my knock with wet hair and a towel wrapped around herself would not have been thrilled if I had just used the key provided and walked in!

Once you are satisfied that nobody is home, make sure you put the key down in a place where you can't miss it on your way out, because you don't want to forget to lock the door and place the key back in the lock box. Many realtors lock the front door once they and their clients have entered, so they are not surprised by another realtor or a curious neighbour who walks in unannounced (I have had both happen to me, several times). This way, if showings are double-booked, the second realtor to arrive simply needs to knock to announce that she is there, as opposed to having two groups of buyers run into each other inside the house.

Unless you have a good reason for starting on one particular floor, I suggest you allow your clients to choose which part of the house they wish to start with. (Some realtors have theories that you should start from the upstairs and work your way down, because people often love the bedrooms and therefore like the rest of the house even if it's not as nice. Other realtors want to start with the basement, as they consider it to be the least likeable part of the house, preferring to finish on a strong note with the bedrooms on the top floor. Still others don't really care where they start.) You demonstrate your style as a realtor on a showing. Some realtors take charge and authoritatively walk through a house, making comments as they go. Others allow their clients to lead the way, discovering the property as they go, and offer comments only when truly appropriate or in response to a question. I normally embrace the latter approach, because I often have not seen the property (unless I arrived 15 minutes earlier than my clients to do a quick walk-through on my own—which is definitely a good idea if you're able to budget that extra time) and so I am not an expert on it (the listing agent should be). Never be afraid to say that you don't have the answer to a question your clients ask! Always let them know that you'll find out and let them know. Such questions often include the following: How old is the house? How much should we offer if we decide to move on this property? How flexible are the sellers on their price? If you try to answer questions without really knowing the answer, you might get away with it a few times, but eventually you'll be caught in a lie and you will lose a lot of credibility with your clients, if not lose the clients entirely.

Always take a flyer, brochure, floor plan, or summary of the home inspection if the listing agent has left these materials for prospective buyers. Not only do they allow you to differentiate the properties when you discuss them later with your clients, but they provide you with reminders and information you may need if you prepare an offer. Plus, they are very handy to keep for a folder of sample marketing materials, which you can refer to when creating your own listings.

When you've finished visiting all the properties you've planned on showing in a day, try to find a way to summarize your understanding of your clients' reactions to the properties. If there are any properties they didn't completely rule out, make a plan to discuss these in further detail once they've had a chance to talk about them and sleep on their feelings.

WHY YOUR CLIENTS SHOULD GET PRE—APPROVED BY A LENDER

Every realtor should become familiar with mortgages and real estate financing. Most people do not buy real estate using all cash, and since they need to borrow money, you should be able to direct them to the appropriate experts and give them tips for financing. Of course, you should defer to a mortgage broker or lender's expertise on mortgage questions, but you should also remind your clients of some important points:

- The initial interest rate offered by a lender is not often the lowest one it can offer.

- Guarantees are negotiable. I currently have a client who owns a successful business with more than $50 million in revenue per year. The business is buying a $2.5-million office building where it will move its head office (they no longer want to rent office space), and the potential lender (one of the large Canadian banks), also the financial institution with which the business does most of its banking, is asking for a corporate guarantee as well as a personal guarantee from the three corporate officers. I explained to the client that he should push back and aim to give only the corporation's guarantee.

- Negotiate with the lender about doubling up on payments, early repayment, and making lump-sum payments—all without fees or penalties.

- Discuss with the lender what will happen if you sell the property and get a smaller mortgage with the same lender (common when people downsize, for example, from a house to a condo). Most lenders will waive some or all fees or penalties if the borrower is looking, and qualifies, for a larger mortgage.

- It is important to understand the difference between variable versus fixed interest rates and in which situations (personal as well as general economic) one might be preferable to the other.

Many consumers eschew using a mortgage broker—this can often be a costly mistake. Mortgage brokers are not loyal to a specific lender, and, therefore, are able to advise borrowers on which lenders offer the products that best fit their needs. For residential mortgages, brokers are typically paid by the lender, and in the case of commercial brokers, where the buyer is often required to pay a retainer or fee to the broker, this cost is often more than made up when the broker is able to get better rates and terms from a lender than the borrower could have on her own.

There are many reasons that your clients should be pre-approved by a lender, but the following are the most important:

- It doesn't cost anything, except for a little time.

- It allows you and your clients to know, realistically, what the upper limit of their real estate budget is.

- It forces your clients, mostly because of the questions a lender asks, to think hard about how much up-front cash, and monthly payments, they are willing to commit to a property.

- If your clients are not very familiar with buying real estate, and borrowing money to do so, it familiarizes them with the process and industry vocabulary.

- It usually allows your clients to lock in an interest rate good for 60 or 90 days.

There have been many times when I have had clients tell me they wanted to look at properties within a certain price range, and when we got to the offer stage, they found out that they could not afford that property. It is much easier for everyone involved if you have a clear financial picture of what is a realistic price range to work within.

A huge word of caution, though: being pre-approved by a lender is somewhat misleading for buyers, because it really means only that your clients have been conditionally approved for a mortgage of a certain amount. The lender can still refuse to finance a property for just about any reason, including:

- Concerns about the location

- Concerns about the condition of the property

- Concerns about the terms of the agreement of purchase and sale

(continued)

- A change in your clients' financial situation, including job loss

- An unfavourable lender appraisal

This last point is more important than in the past because of the prevalence of bidding wars in some large Canadian cities. In 2010, 2011, and 2012, it was not uncommon to have bidders drive a property's price up 10%–15% above the normal market value in a particular area, for a certain type of product. Of course, if an appraiser comes along and reports this overbidding to the lender, the lender will either refuse to lend on this property, or will lend only the proportion they would normally lend, but on market value, which means that your clients will have to add substantially to the down payment they had originally planned.

Since 2012, any of the large Canadian banks require an appraisal to lend on a property. Now, much of the time, if the deal seems to be run-of-the-mill, the appraiser will do some market and comparables research and drive by the property (at minimum, a drive-by is critical to the lender, because it wants to ensure that the property has not changed or deteriorated substantially from, for example, a Google Street View image found online).

Another great thing about having your client get pre-approved for a mortgage is that it can be a tool you can use, as a responsible agent to your clients, to temper their real estate ambitions. It is so common for people to start the search for a house, and when they don't find what they want within a week or two, to start talking about increasing their budget. If you have done your homework (determined how much money your clients plan on putting down, and how much of a mortgage they have been pre-approved for) as I outline in Chapter 10 in this book, then you can be the voice of reason if they start talking about trying to spend more. If they don't have room to increase their budget, then you have to talk with them about reconsidering their expectations (maybe two washrooms versus three, maybe a pool is nice to have versus being necessary, maybe an unfinished basement is actually a plus because they can finish it to their own tastes) and possibly their location of choice. Often by moving a few blocks or a few kilometres in one direction, you can discover a whole new price range for a property that your clients, if they are reasonable, can live with.

To make sure that you understand the importance of this point, I want to emphasize that pre-qualifying for a mortgage does *not* mean your clients will get the financing they need. Therefore, consider how irresponsible it is if you support your clients in preparing or agreeing to offers that don't contain a financing condition. Your clients may not be able to buy the best house in the hottest area, but at least they won't be left scrambling to find emergency financing (which may have an interest rate in the double digits) if they don't have a financing condition and the lender that might have pre-approved them refuses to lend the money in the end. Also, you should consider the legal repercussions for your clients and yourself. It does happen that a seller will sue a buyer if the buyer backs out of a firm deal. And in those circumstances, your client may very well sue you, since you might not have fully explained the risks of not having a financing condition (especially if your client is not financially secure enough to close the deal without financing). Now, even though this type of legal action against you would likely be dealt with through your real estate errors and omissions insurance coverage, your insurance premiums would usually be affected, and you'd have to deal with the legal proceedings and live with a black mark against your professional record.

FIRST–TIME HOMEBUYERS AND THEIR RRSPs

Buying a home for the first time can be one of the most exciting, and most trying, times for a person. Chances are that a first home will be the largest financial commitment a person has made up to that point in his life. To help manage stress and expectations, it's important that prospective first-time homebuyers do some preparation work to help develop a realistic, but life-fulfilling, choice in buying a home.

Self-assessment

First-time homebuyers should perform some kind of initial financial self-assessment. This self-assessment helps to put the potential buyer in the right frame of mind—to judge what is realistic in terms of what can be purchased for her budget. In Chapter 10 I suggest that there are various times when you have an opportunity to investigate where your buyer clients stand financially. If they're not sure, they definitely need to figure it out, and doing a self-assessment forces them to gather information that lending institutions will ask them for, and it also helps the potential buyer to ask relevant questions about their financing options. The Canadian Mortgage and Housing Corporation (CMHC) has a plethora of information and

(continued)

self-assessment tools to assist potential homebuyers through the process of purchasing a home, and especially with the financing of that purchase. These tools and this information can be found by using the useful links at the end of this chapter.

Pre-qualifying first-time homebuyers

The best option for securing financing for the first-time homebuyer is to perform a pre-qualification for financing. At the end of this process, a pre-approved amount is established by the lending institution—this amount should be viewed as the maximum amount. The pre-approval process qualifies the creditworthiness of the potential buyer, calculates payment schedules on fixed or variable mortgages, and helps to establish insurance in the event of potential financial fallout. This pre-qualification process should not make your client think they don't need to include a financing condition in their offers, because the pre-qualification is conditional, often on several factors, including no adverse change in the borrower's financial and employment situation, as well as approval of the agreement of purchase and sale, of the property itself, and of whatever the lender's appraiser comes back with.

Another benefit of pre-qualification is that it normally locks in a set interest rate for a given period of time. For example, if a buyer gets pre-qualified for a mortgage today, the lender will likely tell her that the interest rate offered is good for 60 days. You can advise your clients to negotiate with the lender for a better interest rate than initially offered, and also to have the lender honour that rate for longer (90 or even 120 days).

During pre-qualification, the candidate must verify income and employment. For a salaried individual, this can be as simple as a letter of employment and several recent pay slips. Some lenders also ask for the latest tax assessment. For self-employed individuals, the burden of proof is greater—with requirements typically involving tax returns for at least two years prior, with corresponding notices of assessment and income statements of business activity.

Government programs geared to first-time homebuyers

The federal government, as well as some provincial governments, have programs and tax credits in place to assist first-time homebuyers. Of the various programs available, the most well-known, and potentially the most helpful, is the RRSP Home Buyers' Plan for first-time homebuyers.

Service Canada's Home Buyers' Plan

The Government of Canada has established a program for homebuyers that allows Canadians to dip into their registered retirement savings plans (RRSPs) to invest in new homes, without any negative implications, as long as the money is repaid. The program permits the withdrawal of up to $25,000 from a buyer's RRSP, with no taxation penalty, to put toward a home. This program does have a number of pre-conditions, and they are as follows:

- You must meet conditions as a first-time homebuyer.

- You must have a written agreement to purchase a home or build a home.

- The home in question must be your principal place of residence and you must occupy this home within one year of purchase or construction completion.

- If you have participated in the Home Buyers' Plan in the past, one of the requirements to qualify again is that on the first of January of the year of withdrawal of RRSP funds, the balance that is repayable for the Home Buyers' Plan must be zero.

Note: There are circumstances and conditions where previous home ownership does not change your status as a first-time homebuyer.

Once you withdraw funds under the Home Buyers' Plan, a further set of conditions must be met:

- You must be a Canadian resident.

- You cannot withdraw more than $25,000.

- You cannot own the home more than 30 days before the withdrawal.

- You must complete the form T1036 when each withdrawal is made.

- All withdrawals must be done within the same year.

For a fuller description of the program and conditions, please see the useful links section below for the Home Buyers' Plan.

Tax credits

The federal government also has the First-Time Home Buyers' Tax Credit (HBTC). Details on this tax credit can be found at: www.cra-arc.gc.ca/tx/ndvdls/tpcs /ncm-tx/rtrn/cmpltng/ddctns/lns360-390/369/menu-eng.html.

(continued)

An example of a provincial tax credit is the Ontario Land Transfer Tax Refund for First-Time Homebuyers. This credit allows for amounts up to $2,000. Further details on this tax credit can be found at: www.fin.gov.on .ca/en/refund/newhome/index.html. Other provincial incentives can be found in the useful links below.

Useful Links

Financial Planning Tools
- The Canadian Mortgage and Housing Corporation: www .cmhc-schl.gc.ca/en/index.cfm
- The Financial Consumer Agency of Canada: www.fcac-acfc.gc .ca/eng/index-eng.asp

Federal Incentive Programs
- Home Buyers' Plan: www.cra-arc.gc.ca/tx/ndvdls/tpcs/rrsp-reer /hbp-rap/menu-eng.html
- First-Time Home Buyers' Tax Credit: www.cra-arc.gc.ca/tx/ndvdls /tpcs/ncm-tx/rtrn/cmpltng/ddctns/lns360-390/369/menu-eng.html

Provincial Incentive Programs
- Ontario Land Transfer Tax Refund for First-Time Homebuyers: www.fin.gov.on.ca/en/refund/newhome/index.html
- Property Transfer Tax First Time Home Buyers' Program (land transfer tax exemption): www.sbr.gov.bc.ca/business/property_taxes /property_transfer_tax/first_Time_home_buyer.htm

• • •

As a realtor, most properties you show your clients are listed on MLS, which means you look at MLS listings daily, and send them to your clients to review. Chapter 12 of this book deals with MLS listings, the most common fields, and what the fields mean.

12

Explaining the Terms of a Listing to Your Client

You need to explain to your clients that there is a big difference between the listings they can access through sites such as www.realtor.ca and www.icx.ca and what realtors can access through their local real estate board. The listings the public can see are made to pique their interest and allow them to see what is available in a certain area or type of real estate, the prices, a few pictures, and some basic information. With most real estate boards, the public listings are delayed by one day, which means that only realtors can see MLS listings as soon as they come on the market.

For your buyer clients, ensure that they receive new listings that meet their criteria on a daily basis by email. You may want to review the listings and select the best matches to forward to them. Whatever approach you take, you need to make sure that your clients have a basic understanding of what they are receiving. Each real estate board has a different layout for their listings, but most feature the same fields.

Explanation of Terms

Here are descriptions and comments for some of the most important fields in a Toronto MLS listing (note that I'm using Toronto's MLS listings as an example, because they are quite comprehensive comparable to many other Canadian real estate boards and, also, the Toronto Real Estate Board is the largest in Canada, so this is an appropriate example) to help you explain listings to your clients:

Price: This field always contains a dollar figure, which can be an asking price for sale (for example, $1,250,000) or an asking price for lease. If the latter, it can be expressed in gross or net terms, or as a lump sum per month, or

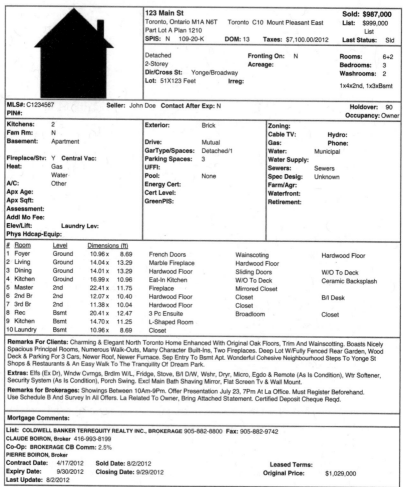

123 Main St		Sold: $987,000
Toronto, Ontario M1A N6T Toronto C10 Mount Pleasant East		List: $999,000
Part Lot A Plan 1210		List
SPIS: N 109-20-K DOM: 13 Taxes: $7,100.00/2012		Last Status: Sld

Detached	Fronting On: N	Rooms: 6+2
2-Storey	Acreage:	Bedrooms: 3
Dir/Cross St: Yonge/Broadway		Washrooms: 2
Lot: 51X123 Feet	Irreg:	1x4x2nd, 1x3xBsmt

MLS#: C1234567	Seller: John Doe Contact After Exp: N	Holdover: 90
PIN#:		Occupancy: Owner

Kitchens:	2	Exterior:	Brick	Zoning:	
Fam Rm:	N			Cable TV:	Hydro:
Basement:	Apartment	Drive:	Mutual	Gas:	Phone:
		GarType/Spaces:	Detached/1	Water:	Municipal
Fireplace/Stv:	Y Central Vac:	Parking Spaces:	3	Water Supply:	
Heat:	Gas	UFFI:		Sewers:	Sewers
	Water	Pool:	None	Spec Desig:	Unknown
A/C:	Other	Energy Cert:		Farm/Agr:	
Apx Age:		Cert Level:		Waterfront:	
Apx Sqft:		GreenPIS:		Retirement:	
Assessment:					
Addl Mo Fee:					
Elev/Lift:	Laundry Lev:				
Phys Hdcap-Equip:					

#	Room	Level	Dimensions (ft)			
1	Foyer	Ground	10.96 x 8.69	French Doors	Wainscoting	Hardwood Floor
2	Living	Ground	14.04 x 13.29	Marble Fireplace	Hardwood Floor	
3	Dining	Ground	14.01 x 13.29	Hardwood Floor	Sliding Doors	W/O To Deck
4	Kitchen	Ground	16.99 x 10.96	Eat-In Kitchen	W/O To Deck	Ceramic Backsplash
5	Master	2nd	22.41 x 11.75	Fireplace	Mirrored Closet	
6	2nd Br	2nd	12.07 x 10.40	Hardwood Floor	Closet	B/I Desk
7	3rd Br	2nd	11.38 x 10.04	Hardwood Floor	Closet	
8	Rec	Bsmt	20.41 x 12.47	3 Pc Ensuite	Broadloom	Closet
9	Kitchen	Bsmt	14.70 x 11.25	L-Shaped Room		
10	Laundry	Bsmt	10.96 x 8.69	Closet		

Remarks For Clients: Charming & Elegant North Toronto Home Enhanced With Original Oak Floors, Trim And Wainscotting. Boasts Nicely Spacious Principal Rooms, Numerous Walk-Outs, Many Character Built-Ins, Two Fireplaces. Deep Lot W/Fully Fenced Rear Garden, Wood Deck & Parking For 3 Cars, Newer Roof, Newer Furnace. Sep Entry To Bsmt Apt. Wonderful Cohesive Neighbourhood Steps To Yonge St Shops & Restaurants & An Easy Walk To The Tranquility Of Dream Park.

Extras: Elfs (Ex Dr), Wndw Cvrngs, Brdlm W/L, Fridge, Stove, B/I D/W, Wshr, Dryr, Micro, Egdo & Remote (As Is Condition), Wtr Softener, Security System (As Is Condition), Porch Swing. Excl Main Bath Shaving Mirror, Flat Screen Tv & Wall Mount.

Remarks for Brokerages: Showings Between 10Am-9Pm. Offer Presentation July 23, 7Pm At La Office. Must Register Beforehand. Use Schedule B And Survey In All Offers. La Related To Owner, Bring Attached Statement. Certified Deposit Cheque Reqd.

Mortgage Comments:

List: COLDWELL BANKER TERREQUITY REALTY INC., BROKERAGE 905-882-8800 Fax: 905-882-9742	
CLAUDE BOIRON, Broker 416-993-8199	
Co-Op: BROKERAGE CB Comm: 2.5%	
PIERRE BOIRON, Broker	
Contract Date: 4/17/2012 Sold Date: 8/2/2012	Leased Terms:
Expiry Date: 9/30/2012 Closing Date: 9/29/2012	Original Price: $1,029,000
Last Update: 8/2/2012	

Toronto Real Estate Board (TREB) assumes no responsibility for the accuracy of any information shown. Copyright TREB 2012.

Sample MLS Listing

a dollar amount per square foot (for example: $1,700 per month, gross, or $27 per square foot net). When an asking price for a space for lease is expressed in dollars per square foot, unless otherwise indicated, it is always referring to dollars per square foot per year. It is important to explain this to clients so they know to multiply the asking price by the number of square feet, then to divide that by 12 months to get the monthly asking rental rate. The field can contain the initial asking price of a landlord or seller, or can be a new price (almost always a reduced asking price, although every now and then you find a listing where the price has been increased from the original one). You know whether it is a new price by looking for a Status (see Last Status, below) of PC (price change), in which case you can look at the Orig. Price field to see by how much the price has changed (again, typically it has been lowered).

District: This tells you what part of the Greater Toronto Area the property is located in. In the City of Toronto, the districts have been broken down into a letter and a two-digit number; for example, C02 or E14. C is for Central, N is for North, E is for East, W is for West, and X is for outside of TREB's districts, covering the rest of Canada. You can also find the location described by a community name such as Annex, Leaside, or Greenwood-Coxwell. It is usually more convenient to discuss location with your clients, as opposed to the previous version of this field, which only had the "C08" format. This meant only real estate consumers who had spent a lot of time looking at listings knew which districts interested them. It also made real estate agents sound like robots: "Can you please start your search in C01, C02, C03, E11, and N05 for me?"

House Type: A description of whether the property is a detached, semi-detached, duplex, bungalow, and so on.

Last Status: This refers to the status of the listing, such as whether it is New ("New" can mean, for example, 217 days old; the word "New" in this case simply means that the listing status has not changed since the property was first placed on the market), Expired (Exp), Extended (Ext), Sold (Sld), Sold Conditionally (SC), or Price Change (PC) if there has been a change to the asking price.

Taxes: The dollar figure listed is the amount of the annual property tax bill for the property. Often this is presented as, for example, "$7,100.00/2012," with "2012" being the tax year in question. Keep in mind that this number may change, as the assessed value of the property will, in the eyes of the Municipal Property Assessment Corporation (MPAC), likely change one or two years following completion of a sale. You should advise your clients that the property tax may increase more than they might expect from year to year. Property taxes do increase, depending on a number of circumstances, but your clients likely aren't ready for a jump of $1,000 in one year. This situation could occur because the sellers might have owned the house for a number of years, and the incremental property tax increases over the years were small. However, when your client buys the property, the MPAC computers will likely assess the property closer to the purchase price, which is often well above the former assessed value, resulting in a sudden jump in property taxes. In the field of commercial listings for lease, this section is often used to show the TMI (taxes, maintenance, and insurance) payable by the tenants, which is often expressed in dollars per square foot.

Fronting On: This section describes the side of the street that the property fronts on. For example, "Fronting On: N" means that the property is fronting on the north side of the street that the property is located on.

Lot Size: Given that properties in Canada have strongly increased in value over the past 10-plus years, this field seems to have become more significant to both realtors and buyers, because the price of the land often constitutes a significant portion of the sale price (in fact, some listings are for land value only, with no improvement or structure present on the land, or, in some cases, the structure itself has no value or contributes a negative value to the land, because it would need to be demolished and removed to maximize the value of the land). This field also allows realtors to, at a glance, know the type of parcel they are dealing with. Many downtown Toronto houses have a lot frontage of 15–25 feet. While many people would consider a lot width of 25 feet to be narrow, it is a huge improvement over a 15-foot-wide lot. Many of the rooms, of course, would be long and narrow, as is the case with many semi-detached homes. This field is expressed in a 15' × 110' format, with the first number always being the frontage of the property. One can also add a word to describe the quality or shape of the lot, such as "triangular" or "irregular" (which often means that the front width of the property is wider or narrower than the rear width, or one of the sides is longer or shorter than the other). The shape of the lot must be taken into consideration, as it can have a positive, negative, or neutral impact on the value of the property.

MLS #: This is the identification number that the Multiple Listing Service uses to identify the property. It is a unique number that will never be reused. At TREB, this number is actually a letter, followed by numbers, where the letter represents the district; for example, C574397. Other real estate areas use just numbers or a combination of letters and numbers.

Contact After Exp: This field is addressed in every MLS listing agreement and reflects the seller's wishes about being contacted by other realtors if the property is not sold and the listing expires. The seller has to initial "Yes" or "No" on the listing agreement when it is executed.

Occupancy: This field tells the realtors and buyers (or tenants) the occupancy status of the property offered for lease or sale, by indicating whether the owner or a tenant occupies the property, whether it is vacant, or a combination of owner-occupied, tenant-occupied, or partially occupied. This information is more important (or maybe convenient) to know than you may think. Knowing that the owner occupies the property allows me, when I'm a buyer's agent, to ask what the seller's motivations are. Knowing whether the seller is buying or leasing another property for himself or herself, and, if so, whether that deal has been firmed up or not, allows you the advantage of trying to satisfy the seller's need for a specific closing date in exchange for something your client really needs—for example, a lower price. Alternatively, knowing that the property is occupied by a tenant, or is vacant, allows you to plan accordingly, and to be sensitive to a tenant's personal space (if it is a residential property), or business hours and employees (if it is a business).

DOM: This acronym stands for days on market and tells you how long the property has been on the market for sale or lease. This is important to know for many obvious reasons: for example, if it just came on the market and is a good property or in a hot area, you should jump on it with your client if it suits her needs. Also, if it has been around for a while, there may be some room for more than the usual negotiating on price and other terms.

Holdover: This refers to a period of time: the number of days after the expiration of the MLS listing for which the seller remains responsible for paying the listing brokerage a commission, if the seller ends up selling the property to a buyer who was introduced to the property by the listing brokerage during the currency of the listing term.

Possession: This is the number of days following a sale or lease deal becoming firm that the seller would like to wait for the deal to close. This number is almost always negotiable, but it is important to note, because if, for example, the listing agent indicates 180 days and also indicates that the property is occupied by the seller, then, as a buyer's agent, I ask the listing agent what the situation is. At first glance, it could be that the seller is operating a business in the building and needs to close it down or move it. If that is the case, it could be useful information to keep in mind when crafting an offer, and during subsequent negotiating.

PIN #: This is the property identification number that the Land Registry uses to identify a Canadian property. Each nine-digit PIN is entirely unique to a property, and this is a sure way to refer to properties, versus the traditional full legal description, which few people understand and with which it is also easy to make mistakes when copying from document to document. I try to always indicate the PIN of a property in real estate documentation. The PIN format is as follows: 122937434.

Fireplace/Stv (Stove): This field can be left blank, contain an N for no, or a Y for yes.

Heat: This shows whether the home is heated by gas or oil (and the type of output, such as forced air or radiators) or electricity.

Approx. Sq. Ft.: The approximate size of the home, which should not include the basement, regardless of whether it is finished or not. If you'd like to mention the size of the basement, do so in the Remarks section.

Drive: This field shows whether the driveway, if any, is private, mutual, or a right-of-way.

Pool: This is a straightforward field with "Yes," "No," or "None" indicated, but it can also be a little more descriptive, because the listing agent can also write "Indoor," "In-ground," or "Above-ground."

Water: This field indicates whether the house gets its water from the municipal water system, a well, or, in some cottage areas, a lake.

Sewers: Most homes in cities are connected to a municipal sewer system for the disposal of used water. It's not unusual for homes in more rural areas, or smaller towns, to have a septic system or holding tank to handle waste water.

Zoning: This area refers to the permitted use of the land. One can be very broad and say "residential" or "commercial," but it is better to put the specific zoning, such as "C4," and explain the uses that zoning allows for.

Special Design: Some properties have special designations that may restrict the use of the building or changes to the structure, such as a heritage or historically significant designation.

Exterior: This field describes what the outside of the house is made of—brick, board-and-batten siding, aluminum siding, and so on.

Room/Level/Dimensions: This describes the room type, which level of the house it is located on, and its size in square feet or square metres. This is very useful in knowing at a glance if there are a lot of long, narrow rooms, if second and third bedrooms are a good size, and whether the kitchen is large or very small.

Remarks for Clients: This section allows the listing agent to write a brief description to show off the selling points of the home and point out the highlights of the neighbourhood, as well as mention anything of interest to a potential buyer.

Extras: This space is used to mention what the asking price includes, such as fridge, stove, washer, and dryer, and if there are any comments the listing agent could not fit in the Remarks for Clients section.

Remarks for Brokerages: This section is seen only by realtors, and may mention items such as easements associated with the property, attachments to the listing, inspection reports that may be available, and anything else the listing agent feels the cooperating realtor should know about the property.

Here are a few of the fields that appear in a commercial listing on the Toronto MLS:

Freestanding: This area indicates whether the building is freestanding or if it is attached to others.

Total Area: This field shows the size, usually in square feet, of the entire building, or, in a leasing situation, the total area that is available for lease.

Ofc/Apt Area/Indust Area/Retail Area: This area allows the listing agent to break down the total area between office, apartment, industrial, and retail.

Volts: This space shows the number of volts of electricity coming into the building. This can be a deal-breaker for many buyers and tenants, so make sure you know what their electrical requirements are. If the property does not offer sufficient voltage for their needs, you can also inquire with the landlord, seller, or local electrical authority as to whether the electrical capacity can be increased, and what that would cost. Of course, you would make that a condition of any deal on that property.

Amps: Explains the amount of amperage available to the property. As with voltage, this can often be increased, at a cost that can be negotiated so it is borne by the landlord or seller, or the tenant or buyer, or a combination of both.

Garage Type: This shows whether the parking is outside, surface, or underground, or whether there is no parking available at all.

Truck Level: This refers to the type of shipping and receiving door. Truck-level doors are the most common type found in industrial buildings. These doors are typically four feet from the ground to accommodate large tractor-trailers, but the gap between the truck and the warehouse floor must still be bridged by a door leveller, or a dock plate or board.

Grade-Level/Drive-In: These fields indicate whether or not the property has ground-level (grade-level) doors. The difference between the two is that drive-in doors are often wider and higher to allow a truck to drive right into the building. Grade-level doors simply allow a truck to back up to the building and be unloaded by hand or by pallet, if the truck has a tailgate.

Clear Height: This is the distance from the floor to the lowest part of the ceiling, indicated in feet.

Sprinklers: This is a yes-or-no field that indicates whether the building or space is equipped with a sprinkler system. It is important for you to know whether your client requires this feature.

Financial Statement: This area allows for the listing agent to detail financial information regarding the sale of an investment property or business.

● ● ●

Now you understand MLS listings and have sent them to your clients, resulting in visits to several properties, and they have found one they would like to present an offer on. But which forms do you use? How do you fill them out? Do you just use the pre-printed fields or do you add flavour to the deal with your own clauses? And don't forget what goes hand in hand with an offer—the all-important deposit! Chapter 13 is sure to be exciting for anyone who feels, as I do, that crafting the offer is the culmination of everything you've been able to learn about the property through visiting it, researching, and speaking with the listing agent. Preparing an offer is about guiding a deal toward where your client would like to see it end up, and I'll show you how to do that now.

The Offer to Purchase: It's a Contract

Writing up your first offer to purchase is exhilarating but also a bit scary. After you have a few under your belt, you feel more confident. You may never be completely sure you've covered all the bases as far as protecting yourself from liability, or that every detail is in the offer, but the main point is that you have to communicate clearly with your buyer client. Some realtors are very well versed in constructing an offer and can do it in their sleep, but there's always a chance that a creative solution may be needed to solve a problem.

This is the point you should strive to get to, because once you are experienced at writing up offers and know how they work and how every little word you use impacts them, then you see that offers can be works of art in how they are structured—and see the evolving creatures they can become as they go back and forth between the two sides, and each change to an offer shifts the deal to one party's advantage or disadvantage.

You've heard about offers being done on paper napkins—albeit long ago. However, you may not know that a property can still be bought and sold on a paper napkin, on a handwritten sheet of paper, or in the margins of a book!

The necessary elements to transact the sale of a property in Canada are the following: the name of the seller, the name of the buyer, the property address (clearly identified), the amount of the consideration (normally money) in exchange for the property, the effective date of the change of ownership (closing date), and the signatures of both parties. So, the sale of a property could theoretically look like this: I, Claude Boiron, hereby sell to John Doe, the property 123 Main Street, Toronto, Ontario, for $10, effective July 8, 2012 (plus the signatures of both the buyer and seller).

Of course, today, the person who would be comfortable buying or selling property on this simple a basis is very rare. Most people would buy or sell a property only with clauses covering a multitude of eventualities, what-ifs, he-saids, she-saids, misrepresentations, misunderstandings, and so on. Therefore, the job of realtors is important, because we take the transaction from that simple paper napkin, fraught with risks and liability for both the buyer and seller, and strive to develop it into a balanced deal, protecting all parties involved. It is really only possible to become proficient at writing up and completing the purchase process with constant practice.

Because each real estate board and each provincial real estate association have different forms, this chapter is based on those used by the largest in Canada—the Toronto Real Estate Board and the Ontario Real Estate Association. Don't worry, though, if you aren't in Toronto or Ontario, because the same elements appear in all purchase or sale documents.

Here are a few things that I feel are useful to know before we get started:

Typed or written supersedes printed. This means that any changes agreed to by buyer or seller to an agreement of purchase and sale (APS in Ontario), whether handwritten or typed, will supersede another section to the contrary that is pre-printed. So, if the small print in an APS says that one key will be given by the seller to the buyer on closing, and you write into the offer, without crossing out the pre-printed clause about keys, that the seller will give the buyer nine keys to the house upon closing, then the seller will have to give the buyer nine keys.

Individual clauses are the most interesting and most powerful elements in an offer, in my opinion, because they allow you to structure an offer to maximize the chances of success (a deal that culminates in a closing), and to get your client what he or she wants.

The offer must be read carefully by the other parties so that any and all questions can be addressed. This way, small but critical steps are not overlooked. For example, "The seller agrees, at the seller's expense, to deliver the Status Certificate to the buyer's lawyer" means that I (acting for the buyer) am not picking it up or paying for the courier; the other agent or his client is.

Every province, and every real estate board, normally has its own real estate forms for use by its real estate sales practitioners. Most of these forms are different only in style and presentation, or they may have a couple more or a couple fewer clauses than others. Here I walk you through what a typical offer to purchase a residential property looks like, what the most common fields are, which sections are especially important to be careful with, and the implications for your client, depending on how you prepare the offer.

Terms and Explanations

I base this process loosely on the agreement of purchase and sale created by the Ontario Real Estate Association and the Toronto Real Estate Board, and work through it point by point:

- Every offer needs to have a date. Normally the wording will be something like "This Offer, dated July 2nd, 2012 . . ."

- The next field is the buyer's name. If it is an individual, write her full name here. If it is two people or more, write their names, separated by "and" or "&." If it is a corporation, write the company name in full, and don't forget to include the Inc., Corp., Ltd., and so on.

- Next comes the seller's name. I always try to search the land registry system (LRS) to ascertain if the listing agent used the correct name. You'd be surprised how often the seller's name is incorrect on an MLS listing. By checking the LRS, you are then able to contact the listing agent to find out why there is a discrepancy between the MLS listing and the LRS. At the end of the day, the owner listed with the LRS is the one legally able to sell the property, so that is the name you should use. The only exceptions to this that I am aware of are if there is an estate or trustee situation, or a power-of-attorney or power-of-sale situation.

- Finally, rounding out the main fields required to identify the parties and the property being transacted, are the fields used to describe the property. The street address comes first, then a description of which side of the street it fronts on, the name of the street, the width and depth of the property, and the legal description.

- In the legal description, many realtors still use the traditional method of "PT Lot 35 . . .," but I prefer to use the property identification number (PIN) if I can. You can get the PIN from the LRS, and because it is unique to the property, it ensures that one property is not confused with another property.

- Now here is the part that most people think is the most important (and sometimes it is, but not always): the offered purchase price. The other elements that I find to be as important, if not more so, than the purchase price are the various terms in the offer, such as closing date, conditions, inclusions and exclusions, and so on. The offered purchase price is a number that you and your client should come up with, taking into account all the information you have about the property, the sellers, their motivations for selling, and anything that the listing agent might have let slip about the property, his clients, or other offers.

- The deposit is what ties the offer together and acts as the consideration necessary to create a legally binding agreement between parties. The deposit should always be held in trust, either in the buyer's or seller's lawyer's trust account, or the cooperating or listing brokerage's trust account. These (supposedly) impartial parties can hold the deposit pending completion or dissolution of the contemplated transaction, and if either one were to misappropriate the deposit, each profession would have an association with funds in place to guarantee the buyer's deposit. When you are representing a buyer, the deposit should usually be as low as possible, but still acceptable to the seller. The reason for this is, should something go wrong with the deal (and there are so many unexpected things that can go wrong) and your client is unable or unwilling to close on the transaction, she will have potentially lost only the smallest possible deposit. However, if the strategic approach is to impress the seller (such as in a potential bidding war or if your client is trying to get a low price accepted), and your client can afford it, then a higher-than-average deposit can be suggested (average deposits are around 5%).

- If there is any additional documentation attached to the main offer document, it should be indicated as a schedule and written in so that it forms part of the agreement (for example, "Schedules A, B, and C attached hereto form part of this Agreement").

- You must place a time limit on the validity of your client's offer. This is often called the irrevocable period (the time during which your client cannot retract his offer). If you don't do this, how long would your client's offer be valid for? An hour, a day, a week? Could the seller find an offer from a year ago and accept it then, forcing the buyer to honour it? Once you indicate how long the offer is good for, then your client knows that he can make offers on other properties once that period of time has elapsed. This element of the offer can be used very strategically by savvy realtors. For example, if the sellers are on vacation, and you are close to certain there is little other interest in the property, by allowing 48 hours for the sellers to respond to your offer, you are giving the deal a chance to be done while they're away. Otherwise, you might have to wait until they have returned from their trip, and risk other people being interested at that time. However, if you get a feeling, or the listing agent tells you, that other buyers are sniffing around a property, you may want to make the irrevocable period very short (two hours, five hours, twelve hours, depending on the circumstances) so that the listing agent does not have the time to shop the offer around. This means that if given enough time, a smart listing agent will call everyone who has seen or shown the property, and let them know that she has an offer that is good for 24 hours, to give them a chance to bring their own offer. Obviously, this would not be in your buyer's best interest.

- The closing date (also known as the completion date) is the day on which the transaction should be completed. This means that the purchase funds exchange hands and the title to the property is transferred to the new owner. This is now completed electronically by lawyers.

- Most standard real estate association forms have space to indicate the listing and cooperating brokerages' fax numbers (I still remember the days when, if an offer was not delivered in person, it was faxed—and it was considered cutting-edge technology to have a 36.6 kbps modem in your fax machine). Many of these offer forms now have fields to indicate email addresses, since most realtors have embraced the speed and simplicity with which offers can be emailed back and forth.

- Most properties have items that the buyer and seller have agreed should, or should not, be included as part of the transaction. The first field addressing this is for chattels, and you should fill out all of those that your client would like included as part of the purchase price, and, of course, any that the listing agent has helpfully written are included in his MLS Listing.

- Normally, all fixtures are considered part of the transaction, but sellers usually want to keep some of them, so you should exclude anything that your clients agree should not be part of the deal, in the area provided for this in the agreement.

- Many properties have rental items (hot water tank, furnace, oil tank, and so on), and the buyers should be made aware of these items and their monthly cost.

- Most provinces have real estate situations in which tax is payable on the purchase price (for example, in Ontario, new construction residential and commercial properties have Harmonized Sales Taxes (HST) payable on top of the purchase price). Many agreements have a field where you can indicate whether the tax will be included in, or in addition to, the purchase price, if it is applicable. If you're representing a buyer, you should always educate yourself about whether tax is applicable for that transaction. But if you're unsure, it's probably safer to say that any applicable taxes will be included in the purchase price, so that the seller and listing agent can catch the mistake and tell you why tax is applicable; or if they don't, so your clients can take the position that the seller should be paying the taxes, because she agreed in the offer that that the taxes would be part of the purchase price.

- Many agreements have a time period during which the buyer's lawyer can search the title of the property, and detail any issues he discovers for resolution by the seller. Allow the lawyer sufficient time to search the title. You don't want to compromise your buyer client on a detail like this where a condition isn't met and a potential sale is not realized.

- Sometimes you see a field in which you can indicate the present use of the property. It is important that you do so, because it may give your clients some recourse if you write that that property's current use is as an office, and after closing, your clients discover that retail uses are the only ones allowed.

- I should mention that the most commonly used forms have a lot of fine print. You need to understand what the fine print means and be able to walk your clients through it or answer any questions they have about it. Some of the more common details in the fine print concern the buyer's opportunity to inspect the property, or how the closing arrangements should be made by the buyer and seller, or how the Family Law Act applies to real estate transactions, and so on.

- Reaching the signature page is a special moment sometimes weighted with emotion. Your client signs where it is indicated that buyers do so, places the date next to her signature, and you, or another person, should witness the signature. If there is more than one buyer, the additional buyer should also sign, date, and have his signature witnessed. If the buyer is a corporation, good practice is to write in the full legal name of the entity on the first buyer line, and below it write "per," and have a signing officer of the corporation sign next to the "per."

- There are, of course, equivalent fields for the sellers to sign if they respond to the offer.

- Most agreements have a field in which, if spousal consent is required, the seller's spouse needs to sign.

- The last party to not make changes to the document (that is, to accept everything in the offer as it stands, whether it is the initial offer, or the seventh round of sign backs) signs a section normally called "Confirmation of Acceptance," and writes the date and time at which she accepts. This date and time is used to calculate any conditions that are linked to the acceptance of the document (for example, "This condition will expire 10 banking days from acceptance of this Agreement").

- If brokerages are representing the buyer and seller, then their full names and addresses should be filled out where the space has been provided.

- Many forms have fields for the buyer and seller to indicate they have received a fully executed copy of the agreement, their address for service, and their lawyer's contact information. This is a simple way to ensure that all parties have all the necessary information to consummate the transaction.

- Again, if brokerages are involved, there should be an area in which the listing brokerage signs, and the cooperating brokerage acknowledges, that the offer constitutes a commission trust agreement, which is governed by the MLS rules pertaining to commission trust.

- Subsequent pages, as mentioned earlier, are typically named "schedules" wherein each schedule should have the primary description fields reproduced: buyer, seller, property address or description, and date of the offer.

I am a huge believer that, whenever possible, you should have an offer you draft or respond to reviewed (when you are starting your career, you might even ask for it to be critiqued) by another qualified real estate professional. Even if you've been careful and there are technically no mistakes (although there often are, unless you are supremely detail-oriented or an engineer by training), having someone review your offer often results in discussions about why you structured the offer as you did and how you could have done it differently. This can lead to more elegant solutions to a goal you were trying to achieve for your client, or to a problem you were trying to solve.

THE TRUTH ABOUT THE DEPOSIT

A deposit accompanies an offer because, from a legal perspective, it is the consideration necessary for a deal to be contemplated. One dollar is consideration, though most sellers won't accept just one dollar as a deposit for the sale of their property, for several reasons:

- In most deals, the amount of the deposit acts as reassurance to the seller that the buyer has the means to make good on the deal. The reasoning is that if a buyer cannot access $10,000, why should the seller believe the buyer can afford to buy a $500,000 property?

- The deposit is almost always refundable (unless you negotiate otherwise, and I've seen non-refundable deposits many times) while a deal is still conditional. However, once the deal becomes firm (all of the conditions have been waived or satisfied), the buyer forfeits his deposit if he does not complete the transaction he has committed to. Because of this, some sellers want a large deposit so that the buyer is very unlikely to walk away from the deal once it becomes firm, since she would not want to lose a substantial deposit. This fear of a deal falling apart once it is firm is much more common in commercial real estate, although much of the time the buyer and seller, and their realtors or lawyers, find a way to mutually agree to kill the deal, or to modify the deal so that it can work, rather than becoming embroiled in litigation.

- If a listing agent has done his work properly and explained to his seller how everything works surrounding real estate commissions, the seller and listing agent will both want to make sure that the deposit will at least cover the real estate commission due for the deal. This is because if the deal falls apart once it is firm the seller still owes the listing brokerage the commission (say 5% of the sale price), because it obtained an offer that the seller accepted. If the deposit is only equivalent to 3% of the purchase price, the seller is obligated to make up the 2% difference in commission to the listing brokerage.

The points above explain how deposits work most of the time, but there are special situations where they do not apply. For example, if a property is difficult to sell, or previous offers have fallen apart, the seller may accept a smaller deposit in order to make the sale happen.

If you are representing a buyer, don't be flippant about considering how much of a deposit your client should put forward. In some circumstances, a large deposit is a great idea—for example, if the property is likely to move fast and you want the seller to take your offer very seriously (or in a bully-offer setting), a larger-than-normal deposit should be considered. I have worked on many deals where a $50,000 deposit is the norm (for example, for a house selling in the million-dollar range), but I've asked my clients how much money they can access without incurring too many expenses or penalties (if they're pulling that money out of investments). They often ask how much I'm thinking of for the deposit, and I ask if they can manage $100,000, because that is a nice, big, round, impressive number. Of course, at the same time, I'm being extra careful that my buyer is protected, either with appropriate conditions or by structuring the deal a certain way (for example, financing and home inspection conditions, review by the buyer's lawyer of the offer or other documents, appropriate dates for title searching, and so on), but the larger deposit is often encouraging to the seller when he is reviewing the offer with his realtor or lawyer.

On the other side of the coin, if a property is not in huge demand and you're representing a buyer, you should be negotiating as small a deposit as possible (remember, the deposit is negotiable, just like with every other point in an offer), because as certain or safe as a deal may seem when you're negotiating it, you can never truly know how the deal will turn out. I've seen very simple deals go sideways, and although I've never had a client walk away from a deposit, I was glad to have negotiated relatively small deposits so walking away was an option for them.

● ● ●

At one time, you would only occasionally find someone selling her home without an agent. Now, in most large Canadian cities, you frequently see for-sale-by-owner signs, and when searching online for houses for sale, you come across listings where the owner is trying to sell without an agent to save on the real estate commission. It's important to understand why people do this, how it can affect you, and what you can do to work with, and perhaps present offers to, people who feel that most realtors are a waste of air who make a living doing very little for their commissions. In Chapter 14, I present some real-life knowledge you can use and some anecdotes to illustrate the for-sale-by-owner situations you might encounter.

For Sale By Owner versus a Full-Service Brokerage

A friend of mine, Paul Gill, was also a potential client and he asked for my advice about whether he should sell his house himself or list it—possibly with me. I have received his permission to use the emails we sent back and forth to discuss this, as I put a great deal of thought into advising Paul and explaining my opinion.

February 28, 2011—Paul to Claude:

Now me . . . I am looking to sell my house in the next few weeks. I have (this week) major renovations in progress, namely finishing off a basement apartment and then a massive cleaning/editing/staging process, but I just can't reconcile the real estate fees? Every agent seems to want 4%, and when I negotiate, it seems to go down to 3.5%, but I think they plan to lower the buyer rate to less than 2.5%, which I don't want to do at all. Ideally, I want to sell my place on my own (like every other homeowner I guess) but is that realistic? I hear you can get a MLS listing for a few hundred dollars, but no one seems to be able to tell me how.

So interested in your take or view as I am kind of stuck!

March 1, 2011—Claude to Paul:

Before I answer your email, I want to tell you that I'm going to write to you as a friend with an expert realtor's knowledge and not as a realtor (if I were writing you as a realtor, what I say might seem self-serving). Hopefully you can trust that I truly believe in what I'll tell you.

To answer your commission questions properly, I'd need to have an idea of what you think your house is worth. Without knowing that right now, I can tell you that 4% to 5% of the sale price is absolutely standard for a quality listing agent's commission.

Getting a realtor to list your property for less than 4% is somewhat dangerous to your own needs and goals. I'll explain why.

Let's say you get a good realtor to agree to list for 3.5%. The first problem is making sure that they will offer the buyer's realtor 2.5% to ensure maximum interest in your property.

The second problem is how a realtor will break even when he or she is making 1% of the sale price, and needs to spend time and money to prepare, market, and negotiate the property for sale, and then needs to split that 1% with his or her brokerage.

I don't believe a realtor can do a good job maximizing the selling price, and the time it takes to sell, with only 1%.

You're correct that you can sell your house yourself. In fact, you're more likely to succeed than most people who attempt it, because, from what I can tell, you're smart, reasonable, and you have a business background.

That being said, studies say, and I have experienced this myself, that a quality realtor will, on average, sell a property for more than its owner would by himself. And normally for more than enough to cover the real estate commissions.

The additional reasons I am not a huge fan of people selling themselves are:

- Good realtors are expert negotiators and often know when to push and when to give. The pushing can amount to tens of thousands of dollars more in your pocket.

- Even though you will surely have any document reviewed by a lawyer (and hopefully one who specializes in real estate), you don't have insurance if something goes wrong with the transaction. Realtors pay a lot of money to hold errors and omissions insurance.

- Sellers often do not realize the amount of time that selling a property takes (even when you have a realtor you're going to spend some time on it, but when you need to be the one organizing the sale process too . . . that will take even more time).

I do want to reiterate that you can do this if you have the time and desire to do so.

If you decide to sell your property yourself, you will need to ask yourself a few questions:

- Will you only deal with buyers directly? If so, you may lose out on qualified buyers who want to use their realtor.

- If you agree to pay a buyer's realtor 2.5% of the sale price, is the time you spend and the potential lower sale price worth saving 1.5%–2.5% of the sale price?

- Will you stage your house for sale?

- Will you live in your house when you put it on the market?

- Will you prepare marketing materials, take pictures, determine an asking price, and find good comparable sales yourself?

I'll be happy to give you a few tips and advice along the way if you decide to sell by yourself. Unfortunately, I cannot place your property on MLS for a flat fee, because my brokerage is a full-service brokerage and does not allow us to provide that service. You will have to find a discount brokerage or specialized service that can do that for you, but again, I can give you some assistance.

I'm happy to talk about this more in person if you'd like. Beer after soccer this Thursday?

March 3, 2011—Paul to Claude:

I did get your email and thank you so much for it . . . it actually answered a lot of questions for me and, in fact, has probably been the best bit of advice I have received to date. So, I am on the fence now on whether to use a full-service broker or a discount one. Do you have any recommendations on the discount one, as I have not heard of any out there? And in your professional opinion is this something I should stay away from and just stick with a regular broker?

March 3, 2011—Claude to Paul:

Like I said in my earlier email, I truly believe in the full-service real estate brokerage model. There are many people who sell their houses themselves, but most of the time you only hear about the good experiences.

When things go wrong or someone is unable to sell by himself and finally turns to a realtor, often the seller is somewhat embarrassed and does not talk about it too much.

As a result, the general public gets the impression that it is easy to sell one's own house.

On the other hand, I am all too ready to tell people about the poor service some realtors offer. If you do choose to work with a realtor one day, even if it is not me, just be sure to select him or her very carefully. Hiring a good realtor is akin to having an insurance policy.

If you'd like, I can look around and try to find a good discount brokerage. (Sorry, but that is a bit of an oxymoron in my books!) You could try and have a go at it yourself (and I can give you some advice and support).

The only potential downsides are:

- The time you invest

- If your house doesn't sell quickly, a property starts to have a reputation for lingering on the market, which can affect its final price and any negotiations you enter into (for example, you're trying to hold tight on a certain negotiating point, and the buyer will say, "It's been on the market for months, I know you don't have a lot of interest from other parties")

If you're comfortable with those things, then give it a shot (and let me know if you still want the name of a discount brokerage or listing service).

I'm sorry I can't give you a clear-cut recommendation between listing or selling yourself.

If it were my decision, I would say list it, but the other option is also viable.

March 3, 2011—Paul to Claude:

I'll probably list with an agent . . . just sounds like a lot of work otherwise. I am not playing tonight (ankle is messed up) but for sure next week . . . can we catch up then and discuss in person?

After that long introduction, which I include because I believe many sellers have the same thoughts running through their minds about selling by themselves as Paul did at the time, now I tell you a little about what it's like working directly with a seller when there is no listing agent involved.

With the advent of mere postings (situations where someone is selling her property without listing with a real estate brokerage—as in a for-sale-by-owner situation—but would like to expose her property to a very wide audience, and therefore contracts a brokerage to merely post the listing information for her property on the MLS, usually for a small pre-arranged fee), which were a result of the anti-competition legislation enacted in Canada in 2010, brokerages were forced to ask themselves what type of business they were in, which usually fell into one of three categories:

- A full-service brokerage that would continue to operate with the traditional formula of listing a property for sale or lease, and negotiating a commission to offer a full suite of services, including, but not limited to, customer service, negotiations, fiduciary duty, advice, and so on.

- A brokerage specializing in mere postings, or assisting FSBOs with marketing their properties for sale. These brokerages often offer a range of à-la-carte services, where the basic package is a mere posting, but, for additional fees, a seller can ask the brokerage to advise him, negotiate for him, assist with marketing or staging his property, and so on.

- A brokerage that offers both of the above.

Commissions and Values

There are definitely some listings on the MLS that are mere postings, although I don't come across them very often and I don't believe they have changed the landscape of real estate brokerage very much. After all, most people are busy, realize that they don't live and breathe real estate every day (which means they are not in touch with the intricacies of it, how to avoid potential liabilities, or how to best price and negotiate a property), and know (or have a vague feeling) that a realtor brings industry and business knowledge and experience to the table, fighting on their behalf.

At the end of the day, no matter the arguments that the proponents of FSBO make, there is one fact that I feel cannot be disputed: realtors are (or rather, should be, as they are only these when there are quality realtors involved) the glue and the buffer in transactions. This means that when a buyer and seller hit a bump in the road, or one side is insulted by how the other side responded, or feels that they are being pushed beyond what they thought they would accept, a good realtor can step in and hold the transaction together if there is still some hope of finding common ground (and, of course, the realtor should constantly be working on identifying and presenting that common ground to the involved parties). Similarly, when one side is offended or proposes sending an offer or response that is unfair or opportunistic, a good realtor's job is to soften the blow, to transform the words or the message into something that still conveys a similar message, but one that is more like being hit with a paper roll than a sledgehammer.

The brokerage I am licensed through, Coldwell Banker Terrequity Realty, remains a full-service brokerage, which means that the sales representatives and brokers of that brokerage represent clients only and do not take on mere postings. I have been involved on the buying side of working with sellers who are selling on FSBO websites (or simply by way of yard signs on their property) or who have put up mere postings on the MLS. Most of these encounters have been pleasant, with the FSBO being pleased to pay my 2.5% commission, because she feels she is saving half of the commission by selling herself. Many FSBOs are intelligent and simply cannot rationalize paying so much money for a realtor to do what they feel they can do just about as well. I feel that they are somewhat greedy and opportunistic (which I say with a lot of respect) because, if you think about it, all properties in Canada have a value that is inflated by 4%–5% because most property transactions in Canada go through realtors, who charge an average of 4%–5%; as a result, the first 4%–5% of the value of a property never reaches its seller. FSBOs are trying to keep more than 95%–96% of the value of their property for themselves. Theoretically, if realtors were never involved in property sales, the value of real estate in Canada would be about 4%–5% lower than it is now, because the cost of our services would not have impacted selling prices.

Because many FSBOs are intelligent, you can work with them quite well if you respect their choice and position that selling their property by themselves is right for them, and if you are helpful to their selling process. An FSBO who put his Toronto condo onto the MLS as a mere posting, and whose buyers I represented in the deal, was appreciative of the professionalism I brought to the table. He emailed me once the deal was firm and said, "I confirm receipt of the waiver. Congratulations to you and thanks very much for your expertise and assistance in execution. I know it was probably more work for you without another agent in the mix."

When I asked a respected and successful Toronto realtor what she thought of the anti-competition legislation, she said:

> No concerns, and have not seen it affect my business. I have had zero calls asking for lesser services for a lesser fee, and have seen very few MLS listings with this setup. I have made a personal decision not to accept this type of business. First, it is not worth my time. Second, I would find it difficult not to step in and offer my whole services in the event my client could benefit from extra advice, even though they had not contracted it; I would feel compelled to.

* * *

An offer is only as good as your ability to read the situation, and your relationship with the other realtor. It is therefore critical that you know how to work well with other agents, know how to come out on top in a multiple-offer situation (or when to advise your clients to walk away), and know how to assist your clients in working through the conditions in an offer. All this and more is discussed in Chapter 15.

15

Tips for Working with Listing Agents, Dealing with Multiple Bids, and Meeting Conditions

Working with a Listing Agent

I realized early in my real estate career that creating a good rapport with the other realtor in a transaction was half the battle toward a successful deal (read: a closed deal). Of course, there are always agents with whom creating a rapport is virtually impossible. Assuming you are polite, professional, and patient, an inability to get along with some agents is usually due to the fact that they possess little in the way of emotional intelligence (although it is then weird that they've chosen to be salespeople); they are insecure or jealous (they should be more open-minded and realize they can learn something new every day, just like the rest of us); or they are simply narcissistic and overbearing (this is sometimes the case with successful realtors who have decided to have little or no patience for less knowledgeable or less successful agents, and have translated that decision into a haughty attitude that filters through to the real estate personality).

My approach when I'm speaking with a realtor for the first time is to be polite, professional, and positive. I also try to make him or her smile or laugh, and drop a few compliments in the first few conversations. For example, if I've shown my buyer client a house that he likes and would like more information about before deciding whether or not to present an offer, then I call the listing agent.

This can be an exercise in and of itself today, because many agents don't include their cell phone numbers on their websites, MLS listings, or marketing materials, and because most realtors don't actually spend full days in the brokerage office, getting hold of them can be very difficult. Half of our industry seems to think they shouldn't provide cell phone numbers, either because they are concerned with safety (I'm not sure how a cell phone number is going to jeopardize a realtor's safety) or because they want to tightly control who has access to them on certain days and at particular times (for those of you who have not figured it out yet, we're salespeople; unless you're one of the most successful realtors in the business, you need to be reachable—not every moment or every day, but quite a lot).

Here are the ways to get in touch with a realtor:

- **Cell phone number:** If you have the number, try this first.

- **Direct phone number:** This may be an agent's home office number or the direct line to his desk at the brokerage.

- **Brokerage phone number:** The brokerage's main phone number must be displayed on marketing materials, agents' websites, and listings. Call and ask for the listing agent. If you're lucky, she'll be in the office, or the brokerage will be able to connect or transfer you successfully (this only works one out of ten times). If that doesn't work, you can have the brokerage page her. Make sure you give them a number they can always reach you at. You have to decide whether to leave just a name and number or whether to tell them which issue or property your call is related to. Unfortunately, some agents screen their calls and messages, so if you leave just your first name and cell phone number, they may feel you're a potential buyer, which could motivate them to return your call faster than, say, if they knew you were a realtor calling about their listing that already had one offer that they were double-ending. In this case, the listing agent won't want to run the risk of you bringing your client's offer in at the last minute and her getting only half of the commission she's already imagining in her bank account.

- **Email:** Many realtors are good about using smartphones and responding to emails quickly, so if you don't reach them using one of the methods noted above, try sending an email and see if they get back to you.

Once I have the listing agent on the phone, I may start by congratulating her on getting such a great listing, or joking about how I see her name everywhere on real estate signs (if this is applicable). Next, I ask questions about the property and gently try to get more information than I'm giving. The more details you get, the better you can advise your buyer on things such as what price to come in at; whether there's flexibility on the closing date; whether the sellers are desperate, or just fishing to see what their house is worth; and so on. At the end of the day, I feel that once you've spent five or ten minutes on the phone with an agent, she is going to better be able to connect your name with an eventual offer. This is especially important if you do as I usually do, which is to call the listing agent just before sending her your client's offer, to explain anything out of the ordinary, if you feel it might help her sell her clients on your offer. For example, if the price is very low because the house is in bad shape, or many conditions have been included in the offer, or if your clients are asking the sellers to leave certain chattels and fixtures that have not been listed as included in the MLS listing, and so on.

It's unfortunate, but sometimes you have to remind the listing agent of his fiduciary duties toward his clients and the obligations he has if he's a licensed real estate agent. For example, I've often had listing agents tell me that I could not send them an offer if their client indicated in the MLS listing that they did not want offers before a certain date and day. Actually, most real estate boards in Canada require a listing agent to present a written offer to his clients, even if it is received before a presentation date and time. If he tells me that his client doesn't want to see it, I ask him to put that in writing so that I can properly report back to my clients.

Finally—and only use this tactic as a last resort because you'll get a bad name very quickly if you abuse it—if you've asked a listing agent to do something and he has refused, and you've checked with your brokerage manager, who has confirmed you are in the right, then contact the listing agent's broker of record or manager directly. At the end of the day, if an agent is violating a rule or code set out by the real estate board or provincial real estate association or CREA, then the broker often has to answer for that violation along with the agent in question. You can understand why the broker may react a little more quickly once she understands one of her agents may be getting her into hot water.

Managing Multiple-Bid Situations

Multiple-bid scenarios, or bidding wars as they're often called, have become much more common since 2006–2007 in some large Canadian cities, where they used to be an unusual and exciting phenomenon. The reason they are so much more prevalent is mainly due to reduced inventory, easier access to borrowed money, and an increasingly expensive real estate market (which can make buyers panic and lead to knee-jerk decisions).

My preference is to warn my clients against becoming involved in bidding wars and to agree to stay away from them if at all possible. I don't believe in them for several reasons, including:

- They rarely end in a win-win situation, which I think should be achievable for just about any real estate transaction.

- Buyers often overpay for a property purchased in a bidding war, and may get themselves into a very tight spot financially if they offer more money than they can really afford.

- The sellers are sometimes surprised by the buyers pulling out of the transaction, which leaves the sellers confused as to what happened and wondering whether they should pursue the buyers legally for breach of contract, and considering what they could have done differently.

I carefully explain to my clients the dangers of getting involved in multiple-bid situations—stress, huge disappointment, and the hazards of overspending or agreeing to terms that they normally would not if they were not in this situation.

However, even if you've warned your clients about the pitfalls of multiple-bid situations, some of them still come across a property they feel they must have or they are so sick of looking for the right house that they decide they'll buy the next house they see that is acceptable. When that happens, I believe it is my job to protect them from themselves. So, if I suspect we might be getting into a multiple-bid situation, I usually tell my clients that we can present an offer on the property, but we need to agree to a maximum price ahead of time and they should be comfortable having me hold them to that top price.

Typically, you know a listing agent is trying to set up this type of competition when they state an offer presentation date and time in the MLS listing. As I mention in Chapter 13, you always have the choice of advising your clients to present a fair offer or a bully offer (which is usually for a high price without many conditions, if any), before the offer presentation date. This forces the sellers to consider whether they want to continue with their gamble of receiving several offers that they can play against each other to arrive at a much higher one or to accept your clients' offer, or at least sign it back. If your clients don't want to present an offer before the offer-presentation date, then the best you can do is:

- Advise them on good comparables so they can arrive at an approximate starting place regarding the price they will put to the seller.

- Follow the tips in this book to ensure they minimize the number of conditions they put in their offer, so it receives the best consideration possible (Chapter 16 is about this).

- Try to cozy up to the listing agent to get as much information as possible regarding the seller's motivations, how much other interest there has been in the property, which comparables the listing agent is using to advise his client, and so on. (Be cautious in this situation, because our industry has become such a game of wits that the listing agent may very well be playing you by feeding you misleading information or lying to you. One way to know for sure how much competition you have for a specific property is to call the listing brokerage close to the offer-presentation time and ask how many registered offers they have.)

- Structure the offer to cater to what is most important to the seller, such as closing date, fixtures and chattels included, deposit, price, and so on, based on what you have been able to determine from the situation and the listing agent.

You can send in your client's offer to the listing agent and listing brokerage or you can insist on being present when the listing agent presents your offer to the seller. When a multiple-offer situation is very likely, the listing agent may request that other realtors and their buyers be in the vicinity of wherever he is presenting the offers to his seller. This is the worst possible scenario for your client, because it is structured to take advantage of buyers' emotions and usually results in the highest price being paid for a property.

If there is no clear winner among several offers, the listing agent often goes back to the buyers' agents and asks them to come back with their best offer, so the seller can choose one to work with. This is a setup for your client to overpay and is a situation you should navigate by providing as much calm and rational advice as possible, to prevent your buyer from making a decision that she will regret later.

I often remind my clients that they really don't need to buy the property in question as much as they think they do. They usually have the time to look for something else, can find most of the elements they like about one property in other ones, and are safer not making decisions while under extreme pressure where they have very little control over the situation.

Conditions: Always a Balancing Act

Conditions are quite possibly my favourite aspect of a real estate deal. They, along with various other clauses, allow a realtor to structure and shape a deal in such a way that she can best achieve her client's goals. Whether it's buying a property for below market price, motivating the seller to replace the old washer and dryer with brand-new ones, having the seller contribute to repairs or to replacing the roof, or even allowing the buyer time to determine whether a lender agrees that he can afford the property he thinks he can, conditions are necessary, but you must be careful there are not so many that they may kill a deal.

When I'm teaching a real estate course, whether residential or commercial, my students can tell how passionate I am about conditions because I get excited when I talk about them. Usually, I launch into a plethora of anecdotal stories and give examples of how conditions have allowed me to salvage a deal, saved my clients from making huge mistakes, or allowed buyers the time necessary to step back and get a big-picture view of the transaction.

However, before I get into how I believe conditions should be used to protect your client, I need to warn you against a worrying trend I've seen developing for several years now. Unconditional offers are very risky for your clients and dangerous for you. Thankfully, they are still not that prevalent, but their use is increasing in competitive markets, along with multiple-offer situations. An unconditional offer is one in which the buyer has not put any conditions on her offer, which means that if the seller agrees with the terms and price of the offer and accepts it, the buyer has no way to get out of the offer, and is committed to closing on the transaction on the completion date. You may ask yourself why I'm against this type of offer. After all, if a buyer is sure she wants a specific property, why should she put any conditions on it? Well, here are some of the most common conditions a buyer might use in an offer (you can see why they can be crucial):

- **Solicitor's review condition:** This allows a period of time for the buyer's lawyer to review the offer and make his client aware of the consequences of going through with the deal, propose changes, or suggest his client not go through with the deal.

- **Financing condition:** This is a condition that permits the buyer time to arrange financing for the purchase of the property. It can be specific, such as how much of a mortgage the buyer needs and which interest rate and terms she will accept, or it can be open, allowing the buyer full discretion over whether she can find funds on terms that she is willing to accept.

- **Inspection condition:** This condition gives the buyer time to have a home, building, or another sort of inspector go into the property and prepare a report based on her findings. The buyer typically makes a decision on whether to move forward depending on what the report and inspector have to say.

How can a buyer, unless he is one of the lucky few who has cash to buy a property, commit to a closing without knowing if he, or his property of choice, will be acceptable to a lender? Or consider a property that looks fine to the layperson's naked eye at a showing, but may be hiding insulation, foundation, environmental, or other serious problems?

My rule of thumb is if a property is in demand, then you should include as few conditions as possible, while still having a legitimate one to kill the deal if necessary. If there seem to be very few potential buyers sniffing about or there is a big problem (such as known contamination), then the property is likely going to be difficult to sell, which allows you to include several conditions or, especially in commercial real estate, a catch-all due diligence condition, sometimes of extended duration.

You should be warned about using conditions, given a court ruling several years ago: you must guide your clients to use conditions in good faith. This means that if you have only an inspection condition in an offer, your clients cannot get the financing they were counting on, and the inspection is very clean (or your clients didn't even have one done), then you and your clients will have a big problem if you use the inspection condition to kill the deal (if the other side finds out the circumstances). However, some would argue that a well-worded inspection condition, as long as an inspection is actually performed, always gives your clients a plausible out in a deal (every inspection reveals something that is not perfect about the property).

Another factor to keep in mind when structuring conditions is whether you want them set up to kill a deal by default or to keep it alive. To illustrate this point, a condition can read something like this:

> This offer shall be conditional upon the buyer obtaining financing satisfactory to it, in its sole and absolute discretion. If the buyer does not deliver notice in writing to the seller within five business days of acceptance of this offer that this condition has not been fulfilled, then this condition shall be considered as waived.

If you do nothing, this condition will keep the deal alive. But, say the condition is worded as follows:

> This offer shall be conditional upon the buyer obtaining financing satisfactory to it, in its sole and absolute discretion. If the buyer does not deliver notice in writing to the seller within five business days of acceptance of this offer, then this offer shall become null and void, and the buyer's deposit returned to it in full, without deduction.

If you do nothing in this situation, then the deal automatically dies. I prefer to use the latter in almost all cases, because if you, as the buyer's realtor, neglect to waive a condition (for any reason at all, even if you're sick, forgetful, or away on vacation), then the worst your client can be angry at you for is losing out on a deal. But if you don't deliver notice as per the former condition, and your clients don't want to go ahead with the deal, then you, by your neglect, commit them to buying a property that they no longer want to buy. Normally, this would incur big legal problems for your clients, for you, and for your brokerage, which would often result in fines, disciplinary action, a strike against your professional name, and an increase in your errors and omissions insurance premiums.

What If a Home Inspection Digs Up a Problem?

Before I get to the traditional home inspection, I want to mention again that in a competitive real estate market such as the one we've experienced in some large Canadian cities over the past several years, it has become almost fashionable (a word I use because I find it funny when people think they are being intelligent and cool when they do something that doesn't really make that much sense) for buyers to do a pre-inspection of a property they intend to put an offer on. The reason I sometimes have a problem with this is that it is virtually only done when a buyer wants to present an unconditional offer, which, as I explain earlier in this chapter, is a dangerous move for both a buyer and his agent. A pre-inspection done by a buyer is usually a less comprehensive inspection than one that is done to meet a condition in an offer. Although a pre-inspection is often still performed by a home inspector, it may not include quite as detailed a report, and the inspector may not have the opportunity or the time to do a full inspection of the property. Its purpose is to give the buyer a sense of comfort, in that there should not be any nasty, expensive surprises if her unconditional offer is accepted by the seller, thereby committing her to purchase the property.

There's another type of home inspection to discuss before I get to the home inspection that most people are familiar with. This one is a full-home inspection that the seller commissions, and the listing agent often has the summary section of the inspection attached to the MLS listing, or leaves a copy of it on the kitchen or dining room table of the subject property, so potential buyers and their realtors can look it over during showings and open houses. The main purpose of this home inspection is to dissuade buyers from including an inspection clause in their offers, and ensures that the seller actually knows what they're selling. This is to help avoid the situation where a conditional offer is negotiated (the condition being of a home inspection) and once the buyer has a home inspection completed, he comes back to the seller for a price reduction, quoting the inspection report for a real—or perceived—deficiency or major (read: expensive) problem.

The inspection we're all most familiar with is one that is ordered during the buyer's home (or in commercial, the building) inspection condition. Qualified inspectors spend an average of two to four hours inside the property, outside, on the roof, in the basement, and in the attic, and then produce a written report, usually using pre-printed forms, divided into sections such as exterior, interior, plumbing, electrical, HVAC, roof, and so on. Some aspects of the report use numerical notation. For example, if an inspection company uses a scale of zero to five, with zero meaning the element is inoperable or must be replaced immediately, and five meaning the element is as new, then the inspector moves through the binder, circling or underlining the appropriate number for each element of the plumbing system, of the roof, of the electrical system, and so on.

I believe that home inspections should be viewed by buyers as follows:

After using a qualified realtor and a qualified real estate lawyer, a home inspection is the cheapest form of insurance you can purchase when buying a property.

The purchase price is negotiated by the buyer and her realtor based on what they, as laypersons, could see of the property with their naked eyes during a showing or open house. Any inspection is going to recommend things that can be repaired, updated, or improved; however, if a serious problem is found (these can sometimes include mould, asbestos, foundation cracks, old or dangerous electrical wiring, roof issues, water damage, and so on), then I believe the buyer has a legitimate reason for going back to the seller and saying she cannot pay the price that was agreed upon.

Once a buyer tells the seller the gravity of the problem revealed by an inspection (sometimes you don't know how serious it is, which is when things get really interesting, because the buyer or the seller may have to spend more money to determine exactly how big an issue they are dealing with), then the buyer and seller have several options:

- The seller is unwilling to compromise on the price and the buyer accepts that she will have to deal with the issue herself after closing.

- The seller is unwilling to compromise on the price and the buyer is unwilling to absorb this new cost or risk herself, so she uses her outstanding inspection condition to kill the deal and have her deposit returned.

- The seller doesn't want to lower the agreed-upon purchase price, but undertakes to resolve the issue uncovered by the inspection prior to closing.

- The buyer and seller agree to some sort of sharing of the cost to rectify the problem.

- The seller agrees that the problem was not known by him or the buyer when they negotiated the purchase price of the property, so the seller agrees to lower the purchase price by an amount that he and the buyer agree should allow the buyer to resolve the problem, if she wishes to do so, after closing.

As the buyer's agent, you need to know when a problem revealed by an inspection may prevent the buyer from obtaining appropriate financing or insurance coverage for the closing. If you're unsure, consult with a knowledgeable realtor at your brokerage or in your professional network.

•   •   •

Conditions are used to protect a buyer or a seller, to give them time to figure things out, or to get things finished on a property. Having buyer conditions included in an offer that are accepted by the seller isn't enough. Many clients need your help to work through the conditions, satisfying or waiving them, and I'll show you how you can help with this in Chapter 16. Once that has been done, you have a firm deal. Clients appreciate having a road map of what to expect leading up to the closing of the transaction.

Guiding Your Client through the Final Closing Process

The excitement of finding a home and making an offer can often over-shadow the more mundane details of purchasing a home. You need to make sure, for example, that your client has a real estate lawyer at the ready—before he or she makes an offer. Some deals can move much faster than you thought they would and it's never pleasant for your client to have to find a lawyer with real estate experience in a panic situation. If he does not know a real estate lawyer, recommend several to him and have him contact each of them to decide who he will use. Once he's chosen a lawyer, he can ask her closing and legal-related questions, but you can still provide some guidance.

Closing Costs and Related Expenses

For example, some closing costs (or related expenses) that your buyer should be aware of (or at least be aware of to the degree that he can contact his lawyer for guidance on them) are:

- Commission (although typically paid by the seller or landlord, sometimes the buyer or tenant pays; you know if this is appropriate to bring up depending on the deal)
- Land transfer taxes: sometimes a municipal and provincial tax that needs to be paid
- Borrowing or mortgage fees
- Pre-paid property taxes
- Pre-paid utilities

- Pre-paid appliance rentals (for example, for a hot water tank)

- Pre-paid landscaping or snowplowing

- Pre-paid income (for example, rental income or income from a vending machine or coin laundry room)

- Legal fees

- Title insurance

Some of the costs noted above will be pro-rated if they have been pre-paid by the seller, or your client may receive credit for them if, for example, she is paying back property taxes for the seller. You and your client only know the credit and debit amounts that are applied to the negotiated purchase price once the buyer's and seller's lawyers have prepared and agreed upon a statement of adjustments, which your client should be able to review at least a few days before closing, and often several weeks earlier.

I should also mention that a lot of consumers, especially those who don't transact real estate deals very often (which means most people), don't know when they need to speak with their real estate lawyer. I suggest that when an offer is accepted (even before it is firm, if there are conditions), you should ask your buyer if he'd like you to send a copy of the offer to his lawyer. This serves several purposes:

- Your client appreciates that you are helping him along by taking care of this step for him.

- You have the contact information for your client's lawyer, which most brokerages will require you to provide to them.

- By putting your name in front of a real estate lawyer, you are expanding your professional network. You never know where your next lead or deal will come from, and as I have mentioned many times in this book, you need to always be promoting yourself—both to consumers and to other professionals.

Waiving of Conditions

Once an offer is accepted—and this can happen with your client's initial offer or after multiple counter-offers—you need to help your client work through the conditions listed in the offer (if there are any). It is imperative to remind your client of the time frame for satisfying any conditions, so there are no surprises about expiry dates. Here is a typical time frame for conditions to be met:

- Solicitor's review condition: August 10

- Inspection condition: August 12

- Financing condition: August 20

- Closing: September 30

Once you have determined that a condition can be waived, prepare the waiver form and have your client sign it, making sure you get it to the listing agent well in advance of the condition-expiry time. If your client has decided not to move ahead with the deal, based on one of his conditions, then you need to inform the listing agent in writing, and prepare a mutual release (or equivalent) form to be signed by both the buyer and seller, which effectively releases them from any obligations in the agreement of purchase and sale. This is usually the only way a listing brokerage will return the deposit to the buyer.

If all the conditions are waived, you now have a firm (or unconditional) deal and the purchase is scheduled to close on the agreed-upon completion date.

Title Insurance

The next step, if you have not done so already, is to ask your buyer's permission to send a copy of the agreement of purchase and sale to her lawyer, who should know about the offer as soon as possible, even if a solicitor's review condition was not included in the offer. This allows the lawyer to prepare for the closing, which includes a title search of the property, communicating with the seller's lawyer, and preparing a statement of adjustments in anticipation of closing. This is the time to remind your client to discuss title insurance with her lawyer. The main benefits of purchasing title insurance for your buyer clients are:

- There is only a one-time premium to be paid and no deductible in case of a claim.

- It protects the buyer against defects in the title of the property.

- It allows the deal to close on time if there are any problems with the title.

- It protects against problems selling the property in the future, if there are issues that have been revealed in an up-to-date survey.

- Any legal fees incurred with resolving insured title issues are covered.

- It protects the buyer from anyone claiming an interest in your land (for example, a driveway easement or a builder's lien).

- It protects against fraudulent mortgages registered against the title of the property.

The Financial Services Commission of Ontario has a helpful brochure on its website called "Understanding Title Insurance" that you can direct your clients to review to understand why they should consider this type of insurance.

You now need to remind your client of the closing costs and closing adjustments that she should be aware of that I list at the beginning of this chapter.

Most clients appreciate a reminder email from you listing the various steps they should remember to take leading up to their closing date, such as setting up the transfer of utilities, cable, Internet, forwarding of mail, and so on.

•   •   •

Buyers and sellers will always need the extra help that you can give them—both personally and professionally. In Part IV of this book, I discuss the various other professionals your clients need when buying or selling a property, where you can find them, and how to facilitate working together as part of the suite of services you offer clients. Remember that other real estate professionals can be wonderful sources of referrals for you.

Setting Up a Network of Experts

Professionals You Need to Have in Your Circle

It is imperative that your client hires an experienced real estate lawyer. Deals can get complicated with such items as reviewing a status certificate, working through why there are an unusual number of instruments registered on the title, demanding a concession from the other side's lawyer, and so on. It can spook any buyer, especially a first-time buyer, if he or she is not completely confident that his or her lawyer is handling all of the transaction details in an expert manner. I wish more people would ask good questions, and think carefully about the answers they are given. As realtors, we can help guide the conversation.

A Real Estate Lawyer

Some questions your clients (buyers and sellers) should consider asking their lawyers are:

- How much do you charge (flat fee, hourly)?

- Do you specialize in real estate law?

- Do you specialize in a certain type of real estate transactions (landlord-tenant disputes, commercial leases, or residential purchases)?

- Will you be doing the work on my file or will a junior lawyer, law student, law clerk, or paralegal be doing it?

- If you charge a flat fee, what does that include (for example, comprehensive review of the agreement of purchase and sale, title search, closing arrangement, and so on)?

- Do I give my down payment to you? If yes, how do I get it to you and when will you need it from me?

- Will you help me understand and calculate all my closing costs, such as land transfer tax (there can be more than one—for example, the City of Toronto plus the Ontario provincial tax), legal costs, mortgage fees, real estate commissions, and so on?

- Where will the deposit for the transaction go and what can happen to it? For example, can the buyer ask for it back any time or can the seller keep it, and is that money insured?

- Is it better for a deposit to go in a lawyer's trust account or in a real estate brokerage's trust account? Why?

- What can go wrong with the deal once it becomes a firm (unconditional) deal?

- What goes into searching title of the property in question?

- When does that happen in the process?

- Is there often something wrong with the title?

- Am I supposed to buy title insurance? If yes, how much does it cost and what exactly does it cover?

- At what point will you be in touch with the bank or lender?

- Is there anything I should tell the bank or lender to get ready for you?

- Is there anything you need from my realtor?

List of Other Professionals

In terms of other professional services your clients need, you must adhere to industry standards, which may be in addition to many brokerages' policies, and always recommend three professionals to your clients for each professional required (three lawyers, three home inspectors, three home stagers, and so on). This minimizes the chances that if your client has a bad experience with a professional you recommended, she will come back and point a finger at you, suggesting you are somehow culpable. Suggesting three professionals places the onus on your client to review each of them and make a selection with her needs, means, and goals in mind.

The following is a list of some professionals that you typically need when assisting clients with buying or selling a property.

Accountants: Mostly useful in commercial real estate, they can help your clients with a plethora of situations and often help save them money. Accountants can counsel your clients on how much they can afford to spend on a property, analyze cash flow, and determine allowable depreciation, among other things.

Appraisers: These professionals specialize in determining the value of a property. An appraisal can end up being hotly contested, because an appraiser may not take development potential into account in her appraisal, and a buyer may not be able to get the financing he wants or needs because of this. When a lender requires an appraisal (this is almost always the case today), the buyer usually doesn't have any say in which appraiser is used, because the appraiser has to be approved or recognized by the lender. Appraisers are good to know, however, because they can sometimes give you a quick opinion, or let you know if your valuing logic is correct or not for a particular property.

Cleaners: If your seller clients are not up to the task, most properties could use a very thorough cleaning to put them in the best possible light during showings and open houses. Many cleaning companies have started specializing in cleaning houses and condos for sale or lease, and your buyer clients might appreciate your suggesting a few companies in case they take possession and the property is not spotless (and that is often the case).

Contractors: All property owners need some work done on their property sooner or later. Whether residential or commercial, you should have a few good contractors to recommend to your clients. There are so many poor or dishonest contractors operating today (almost anyone can tell you about a bad experience she, or someone she knows, has had), finding a good one is very important. Keep in mind and remind your clients that good work costs money. Quality contracting work is not usually done by the cheapest person, but that doesn't mean your clients need to go with the most expensive quote they receive either. As with most other professionals, it is very important to get quotes in writing and obtain several references that you or your clients actually call and verify.

Home inspectors: I consider an inspection one of the cheapest forms of insurance a buyer can purchase. Home inspectors (or building inspectors, if it is a commercial property) should look at every component of a house or building that they have access to (without, of course, inflicting any damage on the property). This includes, but is not limited to, the roof, exterior, electrical, plumbing, structural, floors, furnace, air conditioning, drains, balconies, porches, and pools. In addition to being warned of a major problem you or your clients might not have been aware of with the property, an inspection is a great way for a buyer to familiarize himself with the property he's hoping to buy. The binders that inspectors usually leave with the buyer are a great start for a new property owner to keep accurate records of the property's condition and know when certain equipment and systems will need inspecting or replacing.

Home stagers: Although I cover home staging in Chapter 6, I should mention that having stagers can be a boon for sellers and listing agents who need assistance in moving a property or simply to prepare it for selling. Most properties are much too personal, containing photos and furniture and knick-knacks that restrict potential buyers from imagining themselves living in the space. A stager can work within the budget of a seller or listing agent, and can dramatically increase the sale price or decrease the amount of time it takes to sell a property.

Lenders: A lender can be an individual, a company, a bank, a credit union, and so on. Many consumers approach the financial institution where they bank when they need a mortgage. Sometimes this can work out well, but it does require shopping around to get the best interest rate and terms.

Mortgage brokers: These professionals are normally paid by the lender (especially in residential real estate), but sometimes by the borrower (mainly in commercial real estate). Mortgage brokers know which lenders are interested in lending for each type of property, how much risk they're willing to take on a loan, and what they'll charge in fees and interest rates. Many consumers don't seem familiar with the role of a mortgage broker, so make sure you tell your clients about mortgage brokers.

Movers: Most of the time, the closing of a deal means that someone is going to be moving. As with contractors, there are a lot of mediocre movers out there, and scams have surfaced, so make sure you know those movers who are reputable and can provide references. Some realtors like to thank their clients by paying for part of their move.

Surveyors: Regularly used for land, surveyors are also needed when there is a question as to where a property line is located or if an offer calls for an up-to-date survey.

Where Can You Meet Other Professionals?

There are a multitude of business-networking opportunities available to realtors in Canada, which you may attend with the intent of potentially finding new clients, but if you choose them carefully, some events and meeting groups can have the additional benefit of introducing you to the professionals I mention earlier, which, in turn, makes you more valuable to your clients because you can recommend several professionals whenever the need arises. An example of such an organization is BNI Canada (www.bnicanada.ca).

BNI is an international referral networking organization that was founded in 1981 by Ivan Misner, a self-employed medical practitioner seeking ways to increase business through referrals. Since 1981, BNI has continued to expand, and is now located in over 50 countries, with over 5,400 chapters and 145,000 members worldwide. In Canada, BNI has approximately 307 branches in 6 provinces, with 143 in Ontario.

Members are typically service, sales, or business professionals, such as roofers, mechanics, lawyers, real estate agents, and so on, and membership is limited to one professional per business category. The individual representing each category is carefully selected by each chapter's committee. Upon acceptance, she signs a 12-month contract in which she commits and is required to attend all weekly meetings to retain her position.

BNI is based solely on word-of-mouth referrals, which are generated from other members of a particular chapter. Each member carries the business cards of all other group members, and when a situation arises where a referral can be made, business cards are exchanged. In 2010 alone, BNI members exchanged over 6.5 million referrals, resulting in more than $2.8 billion worth of business.

Another option is to create your own group. It could be a neighbourhood heritage preservation group, a real estate house-flipping group, or a group for people passionate about real estate. Either way, it gives you an opportunity to put your face, words, and business cards in front of people who wouldn't normally be exposed to you, and if you make the right impression, you may become their go-to realtor.

Meetup (www.meetup.com) is the largest website that facilitates individuals' creation of their own groups. Visit their website and search for an interesting local group with an upcoming meeting, or create your own and find out if there are other people who share your interests and passions.

● ● ●

Even though you are a huge help to your clients if you know qualified professionals to refer them to, which makes you seem all the more professional, as I explain in Chapter 18, the people you have to work at getting along with well are most often other realtors.

CHAPTER

18

Building Relationships with Other Realtors

If you are like me, that means you understand the value of establishing respectful and productive relationships with a number of realtors. You can make more money by communicating, networking, and sharing ideas with other realtors than by trying to be a protectionist, seeing every other realtor as competition (which, theoretically, they can be, but rarely are they direct competition to you) who is always going to be out to take your clients or take opportunities away from you.

If this notion has been anathema to you, I strongly suggest that you start regarding the realtor community as a business comprised of great marketing, networking, and knowledge-building tools and resources. One of the best ways I have found to meet other realtors outside of your own brokerage, and outside of any meetings, general workshops, or networking and learning events in your area, is at open houses. If you regularly go to open houses, not only do you meet a number of listing agents, but you meet other realtors, who are viewing open houses on their own or who are finishing up with showing the house to their clients, and you can, in a quite natural way, find some time to speak together.

Another reason to interact with realtors at open houses or other events, above and beyond the benefit of broadening your base of industry contacts, is that you can speak to realtors to learn about specific neighbourhoods or even about a specific property.

If you go to an open house on your own (sometimes there are broker-only open houses) or even if you are the type of realtor who goes only with clients, take some time to speak to the listing agent who is present at the open house. Ask the agent about the house (which you should be doing anyway for your clients if they are interested specifically in that property), or just find a way to get the agent talking. I have found that if I can speak with just about any realtor for 10 or 15 minutes, I invariably learn something.

It could be about a certain feature of the house, which I would not have readily seen, or a new type of technology such as tankless water heaters, macerating toilets, or energy-efficient heated flooring.

Another reason to interact with the listing agent at his or her open house is to learn about the neighbourhood and influences in the neighbourhood, and even just to try to get some information about the sellers. It's good to question the agent at an open house as to why the seller is selling, whether she has already found something, whether she is moving out of the country, whether she is upgrading or downgrading, and so on. Even though it may not necessarily help you buy that house for your clients, it may help you understand specific situations. For example, there are only so many reasons people sell real estate, and once you identify the 10 or 20 most common reasons, you can better understand the underlying motivations. Some of the reasons people sell include the following: a couple is divorcing, a family is growing and needs more bedrooms, a promotion or transfer necessitates a move, or a job loss has occurred. Structuring an offer by appreciating what the sellers are looking for, what their goals are, and what points in an offer they may feel are very important is to your client's advantage.

Another benefit of speaking with a listing agent at an open house is that this allows you to learn a little bit of the marketing and the listing history of the property. Discussing the property with the agent helps you build a rapport; consider everything that the listing agent tells you as valuable information, both for your work on that specific property, as well as your general real estate knowledge.

When you do meet listing agents or other realtors at open houses, always exchange business cards. Let them know that you would love to hear from them, and that you hope they don't mind if you send them any new listings or opportunities that you come across. By doing this, you are going to find over the months and years that you will build a database of realtors. You may have met a realtor only once, and she may or may not remember your name or your face, but if she starts receiving emails from you regularly (for example, a listing announcement when you list a property that you send out to your email database, your just-listed announcement, or an email blast) she is going to be used to hearing from you and is going to keep you in mind when she has an opportunity or when she wants to let you know about a property she has just listed. This can create really nice synergies, depending on the realtors you are networking with. If you build a good rapport with them, enough for them to know that you specialize in high-end downtown condo units (for example), any time there is a lead they come across for an off-market opportunity, or an exclusive listing, these realtors are very likely going to forward that information to you, understanding that if they are of benefit to you, of course you are going to remember them and keep them in mind when something comes along that can be of use to them. As I mentioned earlier, over time you will develop a database of hundreds of realtors, and this can be extremely useful in helping you sell your listings—or, when you have a buyer with a specific need, the email blast announcing your client's needs will reach hundreds of realtors who are used to hearing from you, who will recognize your name, and who will think, "Hey, I may have something or may know of something that might suit my friend's client's current needs."

Create an Atmosphere of Cooperation with Other Realtors

I am always surprised when I hear of, or encounter, realtors who are uncooperative. These people are anathema to me, because they act illogically. They make it more difficult to conduct business than is necessary, and they often cause a buyer or seller to not get what he wants, either by virtue of being so difficult to deal with that my client gives up before giving the property a chance, or, when we have struggled for some time trying to make a deal happen, they put up an insurmountable roadblock, and we then decide we cannot continue to work with that agent because of the mental or emotional strain.

If you've heard the term "cooperating brokerage," you may think that all realtors need to cooperate with others. That is true about MLS listings, where the listing agent must work with a realtor from another brokerage who inquires about a listing, and if the agent eventually brings an offer. However, outside of the legal use of the word "cooperate," I believe there is a vibe one can project or create in order to truly cooperate with other realtors. For example, if I am representing a buyer and call the listing agent of a property I've shown to her to tell the agent that I have an interested client, I make sure to ask the agent if there is anything about the property that is not featured in the listing. If he responds by saying, "Everything is in the listing," I may be inclined to suspect that the agent is not truly cooperating with me. There are a few different ways to look at this scenario:

- The listing agent has an ulterior motive (such as having his own potential buyer and hoping to double-end the commission) and by shrugging off my inquiry, he's hoping to get rid of me. This is truly not serving his seller's best interests, because the listing agent has no certainty of selling the property to his buyer and should be promoting the property right up to having an offer acceptable to the seller.

- The listing agent feels he has a great listing and any agent coming to him with a buyer should almost be grovelling for a chance to be involved in making a deal on that property. I know this sounds extreme, but this is truly the attitude you sometimes encounter. I'm not sure the agent in question is aware of how he is coming off.

- The listing agent does not have the experience, common sense, or intelligence to realize that he is putting you off. Sometimes his mentality may be that he has a property for sale or lease, it is what it is, and if your client is interested in it, she'll buy or lease it. This is truly nonsensical. How can he expect everyone to be so careless or take a risk on buying something they don't know or understand properly? This type of realtor has probably also forgotten that he must disclose anything negative about the property, to his knowledge.

So, when I ask a listing agent to tell me anything he knows about the property that is not included in the listing, part of the reason I do this is to potentially save my buyer money. If the listing agent is smart, this is his opportunity to tell me about something negative about the property—if a problem indeed exists—because my clients, or a home inspector, or I will eventually uncover it anyway. Presenting knowledge of a problem and discussing it up front could result in a mutually agreeable solution. For example, if there is asbestos in one specific area of the property, he could tell me:

> The seller told me that there might be asbestos in one area, so we had an inspector come in and confirm where it was limited to. Then we had an asbestos expert come in and give us a quote to have it removed. We're willing to share that quote with you and your client. I just want to be up front with you since you'd find out about this anyway, and it's really not a deal-breaker if people understand that asbestos that has not been disturbed or damaged does not contaminate the air or area around it, and a qualified asbestos removal company will be able to remove it and certify that the area is completely safe and clean.

Isn't this a more logical approach? Doesn't it serve the buyer, seller, and both realtors best, in one shot?

The listing agent doesn't always realize how powerful an ally the person on the other side of the table can be in helping him sell or lease his listing. A well-informed buyer is much more comfortable making the necessary decisions to keep a deal moving forward, and a buyer's agent who feels that she has a good relationship with the listing agent will feel more comfortable that she has the information she needs to be able to honestly advise her client.

I say this often to my clients and agents, and I'm going to repeat it here because it is so important to understand and practise: I'm a firm believer that, if I can create a good rapport with the other realtor involved in a transaction, the deal is 50 percent done. This relationship is one of sharing information, cautious trust, and understanding the other realtor's needs and frustrations, because we're both in the same industry and only get paid when a deal gets done.

Here are a number of tips I suggest you keep in mind when interacting with other realtors, most of which I have experienced, and a few of which have been relayed to me by other realtors:

- **Be professional and courteous:** You never know when you'll cross paths with the same realtor again, and the impression made on her in the past may dictate the tone of your interactions now. Here's a little story about when I annoyed another realtor without meaning to (in fact, I've been in this situation a few times):

  I got a call from a Quebec couple who wanted my assistance to lease their vacant, brand new, retail condo unit. I met with them and we got along very well (probably in part because I am bilingual). They asked what I would charge them as my commission. I explained that the total commission would be 8% of the first year's net rental and 4% of the balance of the lease term's net rental, and I would be offering half of that to a realtor who brought a tenant. They said they would think about it, and eventually called me to say they thought the commission was too high and suggested another percentage. I told them that I felt their condo would be very difficult to lease and I was apprehensive about offering to do it for the commission they offered, and restated the original commission, which I was ready to accept. They ended up listing the space (at a much lower commission) with a well-known Toronto realtor who does a large volume of retail leasing.

  Four months later, the couple called me and said they needed my help. I told them that I knew they were under contract with another brokerage and therefore I could not assist them at that time. A few days later, when I received a faxed copy of a listing cancellation form showing that they had severed ties with their listing brokerage, I called them back. They said they wanted me to work on leasing the property, but they still tried to get me to lower my commission percentage, although they eventually agreed to my rate. Instead of just throwing the property on the MLS and waiting for calls or offers, or emailing a database of potential tenants and waiting to have something happen (although I did do those two things), my team and I went to work calling every single potential tenant in our databases, and any others we could think of. My team was instructed that, unless they got a "no" verbally or by email, they were to keep calling and emailing potential tenants. We finally got a "maybe," and translated that, over a period of three to four months, into a 10-year lease with one of the top three pizza companies in Canada. Today, my team and I do need to interact with the original listing agent from time to time, and it is the case that he continues to harbour some ill will toward me. From what I can tell, we worked harder at leasing that space than he did, and since the couple did not have strong English-language skills, it made more sense for them to work with me.

- **Be willing to give assistance:** I have lost track of how many times a realtor has asked for guidance or seemed confused about a property or listing, and was incredibly grateful when I steered her in the right direction or gave her my advice. I've ended up doing deals with some of these agents, either because we crossed paths later on, and because they had a positive impression of me, we worked very well together; or, because they felt close to me, they kept in touch and sent me properties and listings they thought might be of interest to me or my clients, and eventually something positive came of the continued contact.

Shameless book plug alert! This is actually the very reason my business partner Pierre Boiron (also my father and the reason I got into real estate in the first place) and I wrote our first book, *Commercial Real Estate Investing in Canada,* together. We would interact with realtors (and sometimes clients) who did not have knowledge in a particular area of the real estate business or who would not understand why we were taking a particular approach to structuring a deal (for example, asking the seller for a vendor take-back mortgage). We would then write them an email explaining a point or a strategy, and given that Pierre kept a file folder for every topic, he would print out these emails. One day, he picked up a pile of 15 or 20 printed emails and jokingly said that we could write a book on everything we knew in commercial real estate. It turned out that we spent the next two years doing exactly that.

- **Be truthful:** Not only are you adhering to the several codes of ethics and conduct that realtors are bound to, but you don't want to be caught in a lie during negotiations, because that may kill the deal. Also, the realtor who catches you in a lie typically does not hesitate to mention it to anyone who will listen. Even if you can't or don't want to share something with another realtor, tell him that. For example, if a listing agent asks me what my buyer's top price is, I can't tell him (unless authorized ahead of time to do so by my client), but I can tell him that it's lower than his seller's bottom price, and that perhaps we can look at some other part of the deal to see whether there is something my buyer can give in order to have his seller come down a little further in price.

- **Do your job of being a realtor properly:** For example, as a listing agent, make sure you fill out MLS listings properly—that means getting all the information to do so. It is important to make the job of a buyer's agent as easy as possible. You want the buyer's agent to be able to tell her clients that the property listed for sale or lease is an open book, that there doesn't appear to be any unpleasant surprises, and that you are a knowledgeable listing agent and have been able to answer all her questions. I have called listing agents and asked them questions regarding the zoning or allowed uses of the properties they have listed for sale or lease (more so for commercial properties), and some have actually said they don't know and that I should call the city planning or zoning department myself to find out. It is not logical for one, three, ten, or twenty realtors representing buyers or tenants to do the work that the one listing agent could and should have done. In these circumstances, it becomes very tempting, as a buyer's agent, to discard this potential property because the listing agent has made it difficult to work with him, has shown himself to be inept, and has basically given me more work to do. If I choose not to do this extra work (although most of the time, I do it, unless it is a property that is very unlikely to be a winner for my client) my client might lose out on a good property, the listing agent may not sell or lease the property, and the seller or landlord may be stuck not being able to sell or lease the property, or only be able to do so at a lower price than he should have achieved.

- **Be helpful and you will be helping yourself:** If a buyer's agent is telling me that her client feels that the property I have listed for sale is overpriced, and I have done my job of pricing the property for sale using good comparables and convincing my client of listing it at that price, then, instead of telling the buyer's agent to go and look for comparables, I ask for her email and send her the most relevant comparables that I used to come up with the asking price. Of course, I'm happy to let her go through the exercise of trying to find comparables to justify a lower price (and good realtors do this so they have ammunition to support a lower offer price), but many realtors do not take the opportunity and simply show their clients the comparables that I have sent along. One brutal fact to realize in this business is that we are hired and trusted to represent the interests of our clients, and even though there are codes of conduct and ethics that we must adhere to, there is nothing wrong with being better, smarter, or more experienced than the realtor on the other side of the table. A person hired that realtor, and that agent is there to protect his client's interests, just as your role is to protect your client's interests. So don't be afraid to profit—both for your own good and for that of your clients—from the fact that other realtors will not always go the distance or do all the due diligence that they should.

- **Act appropriately and make it easy for others to do business with you:** For example, have a business card ready when you meet with another realtor. If you're sending a realtor an offer, make sure you're scanning and emailing it in a format and at a quality that makes sense and is easy to read. I have had agents email me offers that had pages out of order and some upside down. This doesn't really matter if you're going to print it out, but if you just want to take a look at it on your cell phone or computer, or if you want to forward it to your client, you're going to be inconvenienced because, in order to appear professional to your client, you need to move the pages around before sending the offer.

- **Make sure you forget your ego when you speak with other realtors:** I have come to realize that our industry is very competitive and has its complement of A-type personalities, some of whom can be extremely envious and jealous. I have often said something to an agent and had him respond by telling me how long he's been practising real estate brokerage, how dominant he is in his market, how great and numerous his clients are, and so on. My reaction is normally one of respect, and I continue down the path I was on to prepare an offer or a sign back, but most other realtors react to that attitude by responding with one-upmanship, contempt, or anger.

• • •

Everything preceding this point in the book is information to make you a better realtor (or a more informed consumer), but despite my including anecdotes, I feel you would benefit from exposure to more of the *real* world of real estate. Therefore, Part V, the final section of this book, deals with stories from realtors and consumers that hopefully help to illustrate many of the points I make earlier, and also offer you a plethora of tips and advice from real estate professionals.

PART

V

Tales from the Trenches

Real-Life Stories about Deals

Here I collect a number of stories to illustrate how deals are supposed to work, and how they can become complex and challenging. I am grateful to those who agreed to share their experiences.

DON'T DISCOUNT THE GUY IN JEANS AND FLIP—FLOPS SHOPPING FOR AN ASTON MARTIN

by Heather Holmes, broker

"About three years ago, my office paged me with a duty rental lead ('duty' means brokerage duty or opportunity time, which is a period of time when you are either at the brokerage—or today, with technology, you are on call). During opportunity time, any walk-in potential clients to the brokerage are introduced to you, or if they are calling the brokerage, their call is transferred to you. This is a great way for new agents to get leads, especially if they are with a brokerage that has a lot of walk-in traffic, or receives a lot of calls, which usually results if they do a lot of advertising.

"It was two days before the Easter long weekend, and all I could think was, 'Great, another disloyal renter to waste my time over the long weekend.' Renters typically shop around with an agent, search Craigslist and Kijiji, ask friends and co-workers, and so on, in order to find a new place to live. If you can get a renter to commit to you, a successful rental agreement often takes more work than a sale for the payoff. In my first year in business, I did a ton of rentals, and it paid off in referrals and repeat business, not to mention the amount of property I was able to absorb into my knowledge base. But once you get going in sales, rentals seem like small potatoes.

"Businesswise, I was doing well, and didn't need the hassle of a rental. I could have blown it off until after the weekend, or altogether. However, I called him. John (I've changed his name to protect his privacy) was in town only that weekend, I found out, which suited me just fine, but he really needed to lock down a place that weekend. After a few screening questions, I agreed to meet him; he was looking for a higher-end rental and was committed to signing that weekend. As it turned out, we found the right place on the first round of showings, and we closed a deal.

"Fast-forward one year. John's lease was up, and his company wanted him to stay in Toronto on a permanent basis. He was thinking of buying, and called 'his' real estate agent—me—and said, 'Hi Heather, it's John. I don't know if you remember me, but I was really impressed when you helped me find a place to rent last year. I know it was last-minute on a long weekend, and you handled it as if it were a top priority for you. Well, I'm ready to buy a place now, and I'd like your help again, if you are available. My budget is one-and-a-half to two million dollars.'

"I think you get the message."

THE GIFT THAT KEEPS ON GIVING

by Farrell Macdonald, sales representative
at Coldwell Banker Terrequity Realty

"Several years ago on a bright but crisp Sunday afternoon, I was the agent on duty in our downtown office. A gentleman walked in looking to speak to someone. I met with him in a confidential meeting room, where he proceeded to tell me his story. Recently, his friend had died suddenly and he was the trustee of his friend's estate. He wanted to begin exploring the process of selling his friend's condo, which happened to be right across the street. I discussed a few things, but mostly I just listened and told him I would be available to assist him when the time came to deal with his friend's property. I was invited to meet the children who were beneficiaries of the estate. I offered the same confidentiality and professionalism, and walked them through the services I could provide. Shortly afterwards, they called to say they definitely wanted me to represent them. It turned out to be one of the most challenging mandates of my career. The estate went into litigation, which delayed the listing of the condo, but all the while, I kept all parties informed of what was happening in the marketplace and assured them I would be standing by, ready to begin working for them once the legal issues were resolved, which eventually, they were. Unfortunately, this occurred just as the market began to turn worldwide, including here in Toronto. I fulfilled all my promises and worked at securing the best offer possible. Since then, I have assisted each of the children—one with a property tax dispute, one with the purchase of her very first home, and one with both a sale and purchase.

"When I speak to colleagues—especially ones new to the profession—I always get asked if there is any value to our duty roster. I always refer to this story as proof that the office time can be whatever you make of it. I had no idea what that day would hold for me way back then, but I look back and wonder how much I would have missed had I not bothered to make an appearance that day—not just in sales, but in the richness of the relationships I continue to enjoy, thanks to one very unexpected but very special meeting."

NEVER JUDGE A BOOK BY ITS COVER

by Farrell Macdonald, sales representative
at Coldwell Banker Terrequity Realty

"How often have you heard that phrase? I know it sounds rather cliché, but it fits an experience I had so perfectly. I happened to be the only agent in the office one morning when a woman walked in seeking assistance with a rental property. After a brief discussion, I determined it was rather premature, as she and her husband were not actually going to be relocating to Toronto for several months. However, I told her I would diarize her next visit so that we could begin exploring a plan to help them settle into their life in Toronto. And that is what we did. The woman was dressed very casually, seemed rather shy, and spoke English well, but with a thick accent. Since I treat everyone equally, none of these observations gave me pause. She returned as promised, and we began the process of working together. Apparently, she spoke very highly of me to her husband, and we all agreed to meet. It turned out that they had actually been in touch with several agents, but no one had really bothered to listen to them or make much of an effort to truly connect. I thoroughly enjoyed working with them. The husband was, in fact, deputy consul to one of Canada's leading strategic partners, and the unit they rented was a very high-end property. They were so impressed with the service they received that they made a sizeable donation to our brokerage's charitable foundation. Looking back, I'm glad I didn't make any snap judgments (that because of her appearance, language skills, or attitude, she wasn't a serious potential client), but was able to let the process unfold naturally. This couple turned out to be an ideal match for me, but not because of their status or budget. I treated them like everyone else and determined the fit as I would have for any other prospective client. And I'm glad I took the time required to do so—without any quick decisions clouding my view."

ALL DECISIONS IN REAL ESTATE ARE MADE EMOTIONALLY AND JUSTIFIED LOGICALLY AFTER THE FACT

by Joanna Duong, broker at Coldwell Banker Terrequity Realty

"I forget who I heard this quote from originally, but time and time again it has proven to be true. I've had many clients who are very logical in their day jobs (engineers, computer programmers, business analysts, and accountants) that get totally caught up in their emotions, and don't listen to their 'better' logic. For example, buyers who see perfectly staged properties (that may be in a bad location, have a poor layout, or are aesthetically hiding bigger imperfections) and decide to make an offer on a property they should pass over, and sellers who overvalue their property based on their emotional attachment to it, instead of market facts, and fail to have an offer materialize. It never fails to amaze me!"

[Just to add to this story, people hire a realtor for advice and guidance but often choose to ignore cool-headed and rational suggestions, which are really meant to keep them out of trouble—Claude].

IT CAN BE A JUNGLE OUT THERE

by Andrew Wells, sales representative
at Coldwell Banker Terrequity Realty

"I like to make an introduction to my clients that presents venturing into the real estate market as an experience similar to going on safari—it can be a jungle out there! While there are lots of potential pitfalls that can be involved in buying and selling real estate, there is no better protection when venturing into the wilderness than having a knowledgeable guide at your side, with the requisite tools on hand to keep the client safe and secure.

"As professional realtors, our job is to leverage information on our clients' behalf to obtain the best value possible in the current market. To rise above the crowd, an expert realtor goes the extra mile to ensure that they have *all* of the information available that can affect a transaction. Realtors are knowledge brokers at the core, and information is indeed our most important asset. Here is an example of how having information can play a critical role in putting a deal back together when pitfalls threaten to scuttle an agreement.

"My client and I were pursuing a property that was marketed as a legal four-plex with three-car parking in Toronto, Ontario. The three parking spots were located at the front of the building toward the street. The building met my clients' needs, and we believed there was an opportunity to improve the property and increase the rents, so we entered into an agreement of purchase and sale on the property.

"A deal was struck, and after we concluded our due diligence on the financing and physical inspection of the property, we firmed up and waived our conditions. Everything was on track until the title search prior to the closing date revealed that no parking provisions were present in the title to the property. When contacted for further clarity, the City of Toronto maintained that two of the three parking spots were deemed to be an incursion on the city's road allowance, and according to the city's off-street parking services division, it declared that two of the parking spots were, in fact, illegal.

"The road allowance is essentially a right-of-way in favour of the city, which extends from the curb over a portion of the front yard, in the eventuality that installations are required such as underground cabling, utilities, sidewalk expansions, road widening, and so on. The director of the Toronto Parking Authority asserted it had the right to ticket any vehicles parked on the front two spots of the subject property, as they fell within the road allowance, and there was no way we would be able to obtain an off-street parking permit to mitigate this fact.

"The seller lacked any documentation that could confirm the legality of the parking spots, and suddenly the deal was in jeopardy, as the parking spots conferred a very legitimate value to the rental potential of the building's units. Losing two of the parking spots would diminish the potential market rents for two of the four units, and negatively impact the ability of the buyer to sell the building in the future. This was suddenly a very real problem, and the lawyers for both parties weighed in and started firing off letters from each side, claiming that the other was clearly in the wrong. The buyer's lawyer weighed in that this was a material defect and a misrepresentation, and either there should be an abatement on the sale, or we should prepare a lawsuit and pursue the seller for related damages. The vendor's lawyer took the position that there was no claim, that the parking was part and parcel to the property, and with a firm deal in place it shouldn't matter if the parking was legal or not (they also sidestepped the question of whether they bore some responsibility for helping the seller acquire the property without investigating the legality of the parking to begin with). Long story short, the lawyers could not find a common ground, and it was increasingly starting to look like a lawsuit might develop out of what, on first glance, appeared to be an innocuous item.

"We clearly had a problem, but rather than giving up, this was the perfect opportunity to weigh in and make a real difference to get the deal back on track.

"First I appealed to the listing agent to make an endeavour to resolve the situation by providing documentation confirming the legality of the parking spots. He dismissed the request as 'beyond the scope of his services,' and put the onus on his client. Instead of handling the problem, the listing representative sent the seller to the city on his own to try to sort out the problem. The seller was a private individual who did not have a background in real estate. Without a proper understanding of what to look for, or where to even begin, for that matter, the seller made no headway and came away completely bewildered. In my opinion, the listing agent fell short of his responsibility to shepherd the sale through to completion.

"While the seller's representative had already given up, I decided to take a trip down to city hall myself to see what could be uncovered. After a meeting with the zoning department, I was referred to the archives, where I located a complete copy of the development application for the property that was kept on record with the city, along with drawings of the parking area. The approved development application included a *requirement* for three-car parking to be installed at the front of the property, along with a softscape-landscaping requirement. The decision had been handed down by the Ontario Municipal Board (OMB), which is a higher level of government attached to the Office of the Attorney General. The OMB decision overrode the jurisdiction of the municipal parking authority. After sending a copy of the OMB decision to the Toronto Parking Authority, we received written assurance that the OMB decision was indeed valid, and that the city would not issue any tickets on vehicles parked on the property.

"We were back in great shape!

"The buyer and his lawyer were very happy to have the new information in hand. We now knew we could confidently acquire the property without being concerned about any future liability related to the parking situation. More importantly, it headed off what was quickly starting to look like a lawsuit ready to boil over. By this time, we had racked up a not insignificant legal bill, and it was decided to ask for an abatement on the sale from the seller, to offset our concerns related to the parking. We asked for what we felt was a fair amount to cover our expanded legal costs, and the seller was willing to provide this in order to avoid a protracted legal fight and get the deal closed.

"We didn't try to take advantage of the situation, but we also didn't feel compelled to share our findings about the OMB decision at this juncture either. The abatement was a far smaller amount than what had been discussed earlier in terms of damages between the parties, if the parking situation wasn't resolved. Suffice to say, the deal closed and everyone was quite relieved. I delayed faxing the OMB decision over to the listing agent's office until 30 minutes after the deal closed, with a note to add it to his file and pass it along to his client for his records. The listing agent called me back a few minutes later in a huff saying that his client shouldn't have to pay for an abatement if we now had proof that the problem didn't exist. I informed him that if he'd done his job in the first place and tracked down the information to protect his client, the abatement wouldn't have been needed. Since he felt so strongly about it, I suggested he could simply refund the difference from his commission to his client. Funny, he seemed to think that offering a rebate was 'beyond the scope of his services' as well!"

* * *

These stories are selected from many that were offered, and I hope they really illustrate many elements from earlier chapters. Now, in Chapter 20, I offer you specific tips and warnings to keep you on the right path.

Words to the Wise: Pitfalls and Tips to Avoid Them

It isn't possible to list every potential situation that can lead to disaster for a realtor, but here is a list that should give you an idea of the types of things to watch out for:

- Trusting your clients too much and too soon

- Not having proper control of your clients (control can be through your relationship with your clients, or it can be by way of a contract, such as a buyer representation agreement or a listing agreement)

- Rushing to prepare an offer (or any document, for that matter) and not slowing down to review it properly

- Giving your clients advice without knowing what you're talking about

- Lying

- Making assumptions, such as that your client won't be able to get a large enough mortgage, that there will be multiple offers on a property, that the value of the property will go up fast, and so on—until you know something for sure, say you don't know, but you'll find out

- Not listening to your clients

- Not obeying industry rules, regulations, and codes of conduct and ethics

- Not budgeting for the ups and downs of real estate brokerage work

- Not doing your research properly

- Burning bridges—in the real estate industry, like other businesses, you can have your words and actions come back to bite you

- Not advising your clients to get professional advice on topics that are out of your realm of expertise (accounting, legal, surveying, appraising, and so on)

It is important to always think of the potential problems or consequences a clause in an agreement can have for your client down the road. For example, I recently represented a retailer who wanted to lease a small retail space. We presented an offer and when the seller signed it back, one of the clauses he added was the following:

> TENANT agrees that all fixtures or shelves are as it is. In the event that the Tenant needs to remove any of them in order to prepare the premises for the operation of its business, please advise the Landlord before removing any of the items in the premises at the Tenant's cost. At the end of the Term, the Tenant requires to install back any of these fixtures and shelves which were took out at Tenant's cost.

Despite the poor wording, the intent of this clause is clear, and it may have seemed innocuous to some tenants and realtors. However, the consequence of this clause, if it had remained in the agreement to lease, would have been that if the tenant (my client) did not want to keep and use all the fixtures and shelves currently in the unit (left by a previous tenant), she would have had to remove them and store them somewhere until the end of her lease. Then she would have had to bring the shelves and fixtures back and have them reinstalled. What kind of cost and hassle would this have entailed for my client? She may stay in that space for two years, five years, or perhaps more than ten years.

I don't know if the landlord and his realtor had fully thought through the consequences of what they were asking for with this clause. I replaced the offending clause with the following:

> TENANT agrees to tell Landlord which fixtures and shelves it wishes to keep, before [Lease Commencement Date], and further agrees that all these fixtures and shelves are as-is. Landlord shall promptly remove those which the Tenant does not want.

TIPS FROM OTHER REALTORS

by Joanna Duong, broker at Coldwell Banker Terrequity Realty
"If you get an offer very early on a listing (on the first few days of being on the market) and do not want to kill the momentum by accepting and having

to change the status on TREB to SC (which typically deters most agents from showing), you can sign back the offer with all the conditions crossed out (which would make it firm if the prospective buyer accepted) and give them a two- or three-day irrevocable. This way, you would still have an offer in place, but just in case it doesn't go through, you still get the traffic.

"Because most people send the automatic property matches to work email addresses, it is best not to initially list a property between Thursday and Sunday. Friday is sometimes a write-off day at work, as people prepare for the weekend or go out Thursday night. If you list during that period, the email showing the new listing will not be read until Monday, which is a very busy day at work. Thus, the ideal days to list a property on the market are from Monday to Wednesday."

TIPS FROM OTHER REALTORS

by Andrew Wells, sales representative
at Coldwell Banker Terrequity Realty
"Ensure the city is on your side, and learn how to navigate through departments that will help your business. The zoning, building, and archives departments are all great places to start looking for evidence of surveys and past permit applications.

"If you are trying to contact a property owner who is a non-resident about a property you're interested in (that is, a commercial property, rental property, or multiplex), the city will have the mailing address for delivery of the tax rolls. This is the quickest way to peek behind a numbered company and find out who the actual owner is and where they are located."

Real Estate Professionals' Answers to Common Questions

The following boxes feature questions I sent to several realtors whose opinions I value, along with their answers. Many of these topics are covered elsewhere in this book, but I feel it is valuable to include their views in their own words. Note that material included within square brackets and set in italics has been inserted by me to clarify the points being made.

WHICH CLAUSE IN ANY REAL ESTATE AGREEMENT DO YOU FEEL REALTORS UNDERSTAND THE LEAST?

Compiled by the author

- "The acknowledgement regarding multiple representation:

  Where a Brokerage represents both the Seller and the Buyer (multiple representation), the Brokerage shall not be entitled or authorized to be agent for either the Buyer or the Seller for the purpose of giving and receiving notices.

  "This makes sense when you think about it. A seller wants to give notice to the buyer, so he signs paperwork with his agent. Then that agent normally sends the notice to the buyer's agent, who acknowledges receipt of it. It could become tricky when it is the same agent for the buyer and the seller, and he says he's received notice from the seller, for the buyer, when it's impossible for the buyer to have seen or heard about the notice yet."

- "Many clauses pertaining to who is responsible for certain costs or closing adjustments, such as:

  The Seller agrees to be responsible for any special assessment or any other costs or charges relating to the unit as disclosed in the status certificate, or as a result of any changes on or before the date of closing, in the information disclosed in the certificate requested at the time this Agreement of Purchase and Sale is entered into. This amount, if any, shall be adjusted on closing.

  "If something is disclosed in the status certificate, it is usually the seller's responsibility to take care of it anyway, but there still are many listing agents who cross this clause off."

- "The financing condition—don't buy a home without it!

  "In fast-moving markets it can be enticing to remove this condition under the stress of competition, but consider this: if the property fails to meet the appraisal criteria for the lender, it is very possible that the lender may either demand additional equity be placed into the property or refuse to extend financing. It's a perilous position for a buyer to be in, and in a post–credit-crisis world, many of the banks are tightening up their lending criteria. Unless the buyer has either a large down payment or access to additional funds, you remove this condition at your peril."

- "For leasing, every lease should contain an overholding clause for the landlord's benefit.

  "If a tenant provides notice and then fails to vacate on the termination date of the lease, the overholding clause in many instances is the only recourse a landlord has to be protected in the event a tenant decides to dig in their heels and refuses to leave."

WHICH CLAUSE IN ANY REAL ESTATE AGREEMENT DO YOU FEEL CONSUMERS UNDERSTAND THE LEAST?

Compiled by the author

- "The basic explanation of the kinds of services available—more specifically, the difference between a customer and a client."

- "The following clause:

  Seller warrants that all existing chattels and fixtures, equipment including heating and cooling equipment, and/or machinery being conveyed herein, whether owned, rented or leased, are, and will on closing be, in good working order, and may not be substituted by the Seller. This warranty shall survive and not merge on completion of this transaction, but apply only to the state of the property at completion of this transaction.

- "Some buyers think that the warranty lasts even after they have moved into the property for months. I've had some buyer clients come back to me three or six months after closing saying that something is broken and they want the seller to pay for it!"

- "Schedule B, which deals with interest on deposits. Most consumers don't understand why brokerages ask for a fee retainer against interest on deposits. In fact, most agents don't either. It has to do with creating a funding pool to advertise to recipients of interest cheques and remind them to cash their cheques and excise these funds from the brokerage trust accounts. Schedule B is largely glossed over by most agents in my opinion, and consumers don't really understand what it's for."

DO YOU PREFER TO REPRESENT BUYERS OR SELLERS? WHY?

Compiled by the author

- "I enjoy working with both, however, sellers allow me to have more control over how the process evolves."

- "I personally prefer to help buyers because, for the most part, I feel that their intentions are a little more pure. With sellers, it's usually more about the bottom line (although I do know that listings are the cornerstone of building a successful real estate business since they bring in more business). I really enjoy viewing properties and seeing or bringing to light their potential to clients. I embrace the challenge of finding 'the one' or great deals in the sea of listings. I also love shopping, so maybe that explains it!"

- "I like working with both. They represent different skills and approaches. It's fun to mix it up and stay sharp by working with both."

DO YOU HAVE ANY CONCERNS ABOUT THE RECENT ANTI-COMPETITION CHALLENGE AND DECISION, AND HAVE YOU SEEN IT AFFECT YOUR BUSINESS AT ALL (IF YES, HOW)?

Compiled by the author

- "It has not had an impact on my business. My only concern stems from its potential to dilute the integrity of the existing information and processes realtors, as an industry, have worked hard to develop. There exists a belief that agents simply post ads and collect fees and the discount providers only help to foster this. However, I think most people I know and attract do understand the effort actually required and are not interested in handling the process on their own."

- "I am not too concerned about the changes and I haven't really seen it affect my business too much. The people who were arguing for the changes would probably have tried to do it on their own anyway, or found an agent that would practically do it for free, which there are many of in some markets."

- "There are an increasing number of sellers trying to initially go it alone. The problem this poses is that there is only one professional working on trying to facilitate the deal, and if there's a problem it leaves a single person in place to try to afford corrective action. Real estate transactions are integrative—they require parties to work together toward a common goal. Persons who try to sell property themselves tend to be adversarial by nature, and the likelihood that they will be understanding or accommodating is far less than a motivated party with a professional in place to help facilitate their deal. I am aware of one transaction in a chain of eight linked transactions that was an FSBO that blew out sideways on a closing day. None of the related properties closed, and my understanding is that all of the impacted parties sued the vendor for non-performance and damages. It's still heading to the courts, but the seller will likely end up completely wiped out financially as a result of their own actions."

WHICH PROFESSIONALS (HOME INSPECTOR, APPRAISER, HOME STAGER, PHOTOGRAPHER, MARKETING PROFESSIONAL, PAINTER, ACCOUNTANT, LAWYER, AND SO ON) DO YOU FEEL ARE MOST CRUCIAL TO YOUR SUCCESS, AND WHY?

Compiled by the author

- "I don't think I can limit this to a particular profession. I find anyone who attracts the same calibre of client and also prides themselves on professionalism and integrity tends to be a valuable referral partner."

- "A home inspector probably has the most power to make or break a deal. Many prospective homebuyers take what they say as the be-all and end-all, since most of them don't know any better. For example, with knob-and-tube wiring, you have some inspectors who say it's normal to see, it's not a big deal, and it can easily be fixed, and then you have some who go on about the potential dangers in a way that basically scares the homebuyers away."

- "The mortgage professional is also very important—especially when you're in multiple-offer situations. You need quick answers about financing and their backing and support with prospective buyers, so you know if it is okay to remove the financing condition if need be."

- "Lawyers are, bar none, the most important asset to have on hand to facilitate a transaction. A great lawyer is crucial to have for expert advice, and eleventh-hour negotiating if needed. My preferred lawyers are real estate specialists and also litigators—I want to ensure my clients have 'pit bulls' in front of them if push comes to shove."

WHAT CAN OTHER REALTORS AND CONSUMERS DO TO ALLOW YOU TO DO YOUR JOB PROPERLY? DO REALTORS NEED TO BE REMINDED OF THE IMPORTANCE OF WORKING TOGETHER?

Compiled by the author

- "Realtors need to be reminded of the importance of working together. Professionalism and responsiveness tend to be lacking. Consumers need to learn the difference between entertaining themselves and being educated. MLS is a wonderful tool, but most people think that scanning the listings makes them experts on what's going on in the marketplace. In fact, there is an enormous amount of information available that they simply don't tap into because it is not as fun or interesting. [*This includes statistics that help us understand pricing, trends, and how neighbourhoods (or even condominium buildings) differ from one another. Mapping and picture websites and software can allow consumers to get a better big-picture view, as well as a detailed one, of their specific real estate needs.*] Be honest. For realtors and consumers alike, honesty is always the best policy. Be honest about the seller's situation and what the seller wants or expects. For consumers, be honest about what you're looking for or what you expect. I'm not a mind reader, but if you are up front about expectations, it's much easier to meet and exceed them."

- "Be honest and forthcoming. Disclose as much as you can—it saves inevitable headaches, and allows for all parties to be treated fairly. I had one client who bought a house and learned 24 hours after closing that the drains were all shot. The company that came out to survey the damage shared that they had provided a quote to remedy the problem at the same address three months previously. It was an awful experience that could have been prevented, and, had my clients known in advance, they likely would have still moved forward, but would have been able to budget for the work. That type of situation just isn't right."

WHAT WOULD YOU DO TO CHANGE AND IMPROVE THE REAL ESTATE BROKERAGE INDUSTRY, IF YOU HAD THE POWER, TIME, AND PATIENCE?

Compiled by the author

- "Anything I can do to help continue to raise the bar of professionalism and ethical best practices."

- "Have stricter licensing requirements, as the barriers to entry into the industry are so low. In the professional world, usually at least a high school or post-secondary education are required to even be considered, but in real estate, you just have to be of age to get a licence. Fluency in the English language is not even required! It is almost a shame, because real estate agents are facilitating sales of arguably the most expensive investments people make in their lives, but they don't even need to have an education to do so. I feel that it really does affect the professionalism of the industry as a whole, and is the basis of many negative stereotypes associated with real estate agents."

- "Multiple offers—there should be an open and public registry of all parties to a multiple offer. This would do away with 'phantom offers,' and help to instil confidence in the system that actual offers are being made. I've stepped into real estate offices where there were supposedly four or five offers on a property, and found myself to be the only person in the room. This is a situation that could be easily corrected, but there is apparently no will to do so at present in my real estate board."

WHAT DO YOU BELIEVE CONSUMERS WANT FROM REALTORS?

by Paul Gill

What would you like from a realtor (and what do you feel his or her job is)?
"Honesty and integrity, as with any person you deal with in business. The value-add needs to be there as well; in other words, just pulling off MLS listings does not cut it."

Have you ever had a good experience with a realtor that other realtors should aspire to?
"Yes, the last person we used to sell and buy our house. He took the time to filter out properties based on our requirements and did not push us when we were not impressed with a property."

Have you ever had a bad experience with a realtor?
"Absolutely. The worst experience of my life! Recommended from a friend, he was a commercial real estate person who dabbled in residential. He promised the world, but his only strategy was doing open houses, no advertising like he promised. He was even rude when he looked at our house in terms of what we needed to do; in fact, the email extract below sums it up!"

October 6, 2008—Paul Gill to *[name redacted]:*

This email has been a long time coming and is now due. I have had more than enough of your defensive, unprofessional emails, and when you add that to shouting matches on the phone with me and your litany of excuses and finger-pointing, I believe this will be the conclusion of our working relationship.

I understand more than most that I can be a difficult and exacting man, however, we are your clients and as such should be afforded some measure of courtesy and regard. Even if and when you disagree with choices we make, it should be done in a professional and helpful way. I point to earlier emails in which you imply that our house is not "just so" and had we followed your list of suggestions, the picky buyers would have purchased it by now; our house should be "show ready" every day (and it needs repeating); we should lower our price since we are now desperate, and so on.

I do not have to explain to you or anyone else why my house wasn't in show condition on Sunday—I have a large family, one of whom has a disability, to care for, and you have deeply offended me personally (and I can repeat that if necessary).

Now we should offer an extra point to the buyer's agent?—I would rather pay the point (and more) to an agent who is working in our best interest, with our needs in mind and who would know enough to tell a potential buyer that the island slows down traffic and the neighbourhood children come to our house to play because no cars come down there—instead of offering to move it, thus confirming that it is an issue.

I was present for the preliminary meeting with you, during which we clearly stated that our previous agent did not want to pay for advertising, which was why we did not re-list with him. If at the negotiated commission rate, advertising was not in the budget, you should have been up front about it. I originally wanted to go with a full-commission, well-known agent, but needed to confirm that you would provide the same service for less commission in order to get me to agree.

I would like you to sign a termination of our contract, and I hope you do the right thing because things have broken down irreparably and I think your previous issues with me are affecting your attitude. If you refuse, then I will let the listing expire rather than continue this relationship, which so clearly is not working for any of us. I am sure we don't want this to get any nastier or go any further than it already has.

Please come and get your sign off my lawn.

Paul Gill

WHAT DO YOU BELIEVE CONSUMERS WANT FROM REALTORS?

by Shawn Bedard

What would you like from a realtor (and what do you feel his or her job is)?
"What I'd like in a realtor is expertise and knowledge in the types of real estate and area that I'm looking in. I feel their job is to understand the needs of the client, the area, and what would work best for the client. The realtor knows what questions to ask to draw out the information they need to provide the right advice."

Have you ever had a good experience with a realtor that other realtors should aspire to?
"I had a good experience with Pierre [*Boiron*]. Although he gets compensated by making a deal for me to buy a property, he provides honest and candid advice when a property is not right for my interests. This is very much appreciated."

Have you ever had a bad experience with a realtor?
"Mostly from realtors on the other side [*on the other side of the negotiating table*]. When the realtor is not responsive, fails to provide necessary information, and has trouble communicating simple details it's often difficult to work with them."

WHAT DO YOU BELIEVE CONSUMERS WANT FROM REALTORS?

by Paul Grissom

Who is your favourite real estate agent?
"I would give the prize to agents we worked with, who I refer to here as Andrew and Linda. They specialize in the Beaches area of Toronto, where I've lived for about 30 years. They win for their professionalism in dealing with us as clients over the years.

"My wife, Annie, met 'Andrew' on one of her open house snoopings. She likes to do that even though we're not about to move. Andrew must have asked some pretty good questions because it wasn't long before he was showing us houses very much to our taste in areas we aspired to. He had an uncanny understanding of what we would like, and even though it was clear we weren't about to move for a long time, he house hunted with us for close to five years. It was a real education. He showed me how to spot mechanical deficiencies, a problem basement, and other typical problems of older homes in the area. Did you know the Beaches area is laced by underground streams, some of which run right up against the foundations of homes on certain streets?

"Over the years we began to view these agents as our personal real estate agents. Then came a day when Annie found 'the house.' She'd noticed one of their signs on a tree-lined street she'd been watching and paid a visit. Shortly after, I was dragged kicking and screaming to see it. (I was not looking to move at the time.)

"I don't recall 'Linda' saying anything—the marble fireplace details, the 100-year-old pine woodwork, the modern kitchen and the sky-lit studio said it all. Within a day or two of talking it over, we made our offer. After a day of back-and-forthing, the house was ours.

"Now, everyone knows you should sell first and then buy, but we were caught up in the emotion of the moment and didn't care. Besides, Linda had seen our house and already knew she had a buyer for it—a young couple, perfect for our little two-bedroom farmhouse. Our price was no problem and the deal was done within three hours.

"Andrew and Linda made everything smooth and easy for us. I suppose we were the ideal clients because we took their advice in both transactions. Why? Because after years of working with us, they had earned our trust. They took the trouble to get to know us; they never wasted our time or made us feel like we were squandering theirs.

"The outcome was happy for all. Andrew and Linda take a genuine interest in their prospects and they take the time to build relationships. They were generous with their time and information, and I gather from talking to other agents in the area that they don't treat them as competition, but as peers. They cooperate with them, to everyone's advantage.

"Linda still visits now and then for coffee and to talk real estate. We're getting on in years and we'll downsize someday. She knows that, and she doesn't look upon a sale as an end; she sees it as the beginning of the next sale.

Who is your least favourite real estate agent?
"I don't have one. But I'll tell you about a perfectly good guy who blew it with me. I was on the hunt for a cottage, and while fishing with a buddy one weekend, just happened to spot an agent's sign from the water of Percy's Reach on the Trent Canal. We wanted only to get an idea of what you get for the money in that area as a kind of benchmark, and we told the agent so.

"That first property was in no way what we were looking for, but he seemed not to get this fact. After two or three more tries, we found ourselves in a place that was nice and was relatively isolated, which mattered to us because we didn't want to be cheek by jowl with neighbours. I told him so, but also said that I wasn't sure about the place. We returned to the city.

"That week, he phoned and said he would be in Toronto and could he stop at my office and say hello? Of course he could! But when he arrived, he had an offer of purchase and sale that he plunked down in front of me suggesting I should get off the fence and sign, because it was so right for me.

"He did two things very wrong. He misread my interest and he tried to push me into signing. It was a bit embarrassing, but I had to tell him I was just not that hot for the property. We parted cordially, vowing to keep in touch, and I never had another word with him."

WHAT DO YOU BELIEVE CONSUMERS WANT FROM REALTORS?

by Gerald Moodie

What would you like from a realtor and what do you feel his or her job is?
"When purchasing I require a realtor who is an experienced adviser and consultant. I want a realtor who understands the market and can show me properties that are closely aligned with what I am looking for—a good realtor spends time with me to identify my needs, wants, and desires before we begin to look at properties. The best realtors help define and refine what I am looking for, and can present me with options that I would not have considered on my own; they know the boundaries but are not afraid to push them. A good realtor adds value to the process and the relationship. They provide solid advice on market trends, neighbourhoods, builders, quality of construction and pricing, and act as a voice of rational second thought to eliminate the counterproductive emotions that are normally involved in real estate purchases. In a perfect world, a

good realtor will show me properties that are exceptional deals, or are unique, or both. I also want a realtor who personally knows exceptional industry professionals, such as mortgage brokers, bankers, contractors, property inspectors, insurance brokers, and so on, and feels comfortable recommending them.

"When selling, I want a realtor who is an aggressive sales-and-marketing professional. I want a realtor who has the ability to show my property in the very best light and can attract qualified buyers using a well-developed professional network and a broad range of media. A good realtor will be able to inform me who my purchaser will be, their demographic, salary, and what they will be looking for most. If work needs to be done to my property in preparation for the sale, I want a realtor who can tell me exactly what needs to be done and recommend exceptional professionals who are reasonably priced and will only do what has to be done. I need a realtor who will not give up easily and is as determined to get the best price for my property as I am. A good realtor has the confidence and knowledge to tell me what I need to know."

Have you ever had a good experience with a realtor that other realtors should aspire to?

"I worked with a realtor by the name of Peter Thompson when I first began investing in real estate. Peter was a successful private real estate investor who decided to get his licence and understood the psychology of real estate investing and the need to maintain momentum once a good deal was identified. He knew the markets exceptionally well, and knew which properties would likely appreciate most. In addition, he had an exceptional network of friends who were developers, city planners, bankers, and investors that he knew from having grown up in Lawrence Park, and he drew upon these sources constantly for valuable information. Peter was a pit bull when a good deal became available. He knew the numbers from every perspective, and when they made sense, he would not let the deal collapse. He understood that I was new to real estate investing and that I had a natural tendency to avoid risk, so he would gently push me forward despite myself. At the time, I had a good job but limited capital; however, Peter had connections in mortgage financing and I ended up with four mortgages, including a 0% vendor take-back, to structure my first deal. At the time, I was terrified, but Peter assured me that the neighbourhoods between Lawrence and Eglinton near Yonge Street were going to do well, and that I would thank him one day. Peter and I remain the best of friends and I do thank him every time I see him."

Have you ever had a bad experience with a realtor?
"I have never dealt with a bad realtor, but I have dealt with a bad real estate lawyer. I once purchased a property and found out three years later, when we went to sell the property, that the title had never been registered."

WHAT DO YOU BELIEVE CONSUMERS WANT FROM REALTORS?

by Maciek Tarnowski

What would you like from a realtor and what do you feel his or her job is?
"Experience, knowledge, bargaining ability, communication, making clients feel like they're number one."

Have you ever had a good experience with a realtor that other realtors should aspire to?
"Selling our condo (with not many days left to do so) in a time when everyone was weary of real estate—that was dramatic—but it did get done, which is the good story. And buying our house—letters in everyone's mailbox in the neigh-bourhood was a nice touch, and got the results that everyone was happy with."

Have you ever had a bad experience with a realtor?
"My grandmother hired a friend's daughter—her first experience after getting her real estate licence. The house took a long time to sell and the experience was stressful. She didn't get close to the asking price at all. There was no counselling on what to do around the house to make it saleable."

Appendix A

Helpful Tools and Further Reading

Financial planning tools:
- The Canadian Mortgage and Housing Corporation: www.cmhc-schl .gc.ca/en/index.cfm
- The Financial Consumer Agency of Canada: www.fcac-acfc.gc.ca /eng/index-eng.asp

Federal incentive programs:
- Home Buyers' Plan: www.cra-arc.gc.ca/tx/ndvdls/tpcs/rrsp-reer /hbp-rap/menu-eng.html
- First-time Home Buyers' Tax Credit: www.cra-arc.gc.ca/tx/ndvdls /tpcs/ncm-tx/rtrn/cmpltng/ddctns/lns360-390/369/menu-eng.html

Marketing tools:
- Corefuel: www.corefuel.com
- Facebook: www.facebook.com
- LinkedIn: www.linkedin.com/home
- Real Web Solutions: www.realwebsolutions.com
- Real Estate Webmasters: www.realestatewebmasters.com
- Twitter: www.twitter.com

Real estate associations:
- Alberta Real Estate Association: www.areahub.ca
- British Columbia Real Estate Association: www.bcrea.bc.ca

- Manitoba Real Estate Association: www.realestatemanitoba.com
- Organisme d'autoréglementation du courtage immobilier du Québec: www.oaciq.com/en
- Ontario Real Estate Association: www.orea.com
- New Brunswick Real Estate Association: www.nbrea.ca
- Nova Scotia Real Estate Commission: www.nsrec.ns.ca
- Prince Edward Island Real Estate Association: www.peirea.com
- Newfoundland and Labrador Association of REALTORS®: boards.mls.ca/nl
- Real Estate Council of Ontario: www.reco.on.ca
- REALTOR.ca—commercial properties: www.icx.ca
- REALTOR.ca—residential properties: www.realtor.ca (the new www.mls.ca)
- Association of Saskatchewan REALTORS®: www.saskatchewanreal estate.com
- Toronto Real Estate Board: www.torontorealestateboard.com
- Yellowknife Real Estate Board: boards.mls.ca/yellowknife
- Yukon Real Estate Association: www.yrea.ca

Provincial incentive programs:
- Ontario Land Transfer Tax Refund for First-Time Homebuyers: www.fin.gov.on.ca/en/refund/newhome/index.html
- British Columbia Property Transfer Tax First Time Home Buyers' Program: www.sbr.gov.bc.ca/business/property_taxes/property _transfer_tax/first_Time_home_buyer.htm

Appendix B

Glossary

Accepted offer: This is an offer that has been accepted as is, without any modification by the receiving party. For example, a seller can accept a buyer's initial offer or a buyer can accept the seller's counter-offer after several sign backs. An accepted offer can be conditional or unconditional.

Builder: The person or company that either arranges through contractors and sub-contractors the physical work of improving a piece of land (such as erecting a house, building, condo building, and so on) or does the work himself or itself.

Buyer: This is the person or entity purchasing a property. Much of the time in the real estate brokerage industry, the term "buyer" is synonymous with "tenant." A buyer can be an individual, several people, or a corporation, and can also be buying in trust.

Buyer's agent (or selling agent): This is the agent who represents the buyer. (It is admittedly confusing that this person is also known as the *selling* agent, when it's the buyer they are working for.)

Closing (of a transaction): When the purchase or lease of a property takes effect. With sales, this is the day when the title changes hands, as does the money.

Closing (sales terminology): This is from the typical sales vernacular, where a salesperson is supposed to be trying to close the deal with a client, as in the phrase, "always be closing."

Commission: This can be a flat rate or a percentage of the purchase price or lease rate. Typically, it is paid by the seller or landlord to the listing brokerage, which in turn pays part of it to the brokerage representing the buyer or tenant.

Commission split: The split between the brokerage and its agent working on a specific transaction.

Comparables: Comparables are properties that have sold and are, preferably, very similar to the subject property in as many aspects as possible, such as geographic location, size, view, neighbourhood influences, amenities, age, type and quality of finishes, quality of construction, and so on.

Conditional deal (or conditionally accepted offer): An accepted offer that contains conditions.

Conditional offer: An offer that is being made with conditions. If accepted by the other party with the conditions, it becomes a conditional deal.

Cooperating brokerage (or selling brokerage): This is the brokerage representing the tenant or buyer.

CREA: The acronym for the Canadian Real Estate Association (www.crea.ca).

Curb appeal: The appeal of a property to potential buyers or tenants, as viewed from the exterior. This can often be improved by beautifying the property, repairing any broken elements, quality landscaping, and so on.

Developer: This is a catch-all term that can include a person or a company that renovates properties and leases or sells them, as well as one that takes land through the development approval process in order to build on the land or sell it to a builder. Developers are known as people who take ideas and convert them into real properties.

Expiry date: In the real estate industry, there are several expiry dates, including the expiry of an irrevocable period, but the most important is normally the expiry of a condition, since it needs to be waived or reported as fulfilled, or the deal will otherwise die.

Firm deal: A deal where there are no conditions. An accepted deal can be firm right off the bat if there are no conditions, or a conditional deal can have its conditions waived or satisfied and become a firm deal. From the point when a deal becomes firm, there is normally no more negotiating between the parties, but, rather, both sides start making their respective arrangements for the upcoming closing.

Flip: Buying a property with the intention of reselling for a profit. This can be done quickly if the property is bought sufficiently under market value, or can be done once renovations or other improvements have been made to increase the value of the property.

High efficiency: Used to indicate that appliances, hot water tanks, furnaces, air-conditioning units, or HVAC units consume less energy or water to do the same thing as other units.

IDX feed: Internet data exchange feed, an electronic feed used by the real estate industry to allow people to conduct their own searches of the MLS listings in their area.

Irrevocable period: The period of time during which the buyer or seller (whichever made the last offer) cannot revoke his offer. This can be used as a negotiation tool, because the buyer or seller may not want to risk losing the deal by delaying making a decision. For example, if a buyer puts a two-hour irrevocable period in his initial offer, and the seller has an open house in five hours, the seller has to make the decision of accepting or working with that buyer's offer or take the risk of hoping to attract better offers from visitors to her open house.

Knob-and-tube: An old type of electrical wiring that is shunned because of its greater potential to start fires, as it lacks a grounding conductor. This is one element that home inspections reveal, and insurance companies usually do not insure homes unless they are upgraded to modern electrical wiring.

Landlord: The owner of a rental property or space.

LEED: The acronym for Leadership in Energy and Environmental Design, a range of rating systems for the creation, construction, and ongoing operation of green buildings, houses, and even neighbourhoods.

Listing: A brokerage's mandate from a seller or landlord to sell or lease her property.

Listing agent: The realtor who markets a seller's or landlord's property for lease or sale on behalf of the listing brokerage.

Listing brokerage: The entity that a seller or landlord contracts to sell or lease his property.

MLS: This acronym stands for Multiple Listing Service (www.realtor.ca).

OREA: The acronym for the Ontario Real Estate Association (www.orea.com).

Parquet flooring: Although the current fad is modern wood flooring, parquet flooring has long been appreciated for its geometric appeal, and was used extensively in hallways and bedrooms because it is warmer than tiles but easier to keep clean than broadloom. Older clients may appreciate houses or condo units with parquet flooring in good condition.

Realtor: The term "realtor" refers to brokers and sales representatives who are members of The Canadian Real Estate Association and who accept and respect a strict code of ethics, and who are required to meet consistent professional standards of business practice—which is the consumer's assurance of integrity.

RECO: The acronym for the Real Estate Council of Ontario (www.reco.on.ca).

Renovation: Improving a building, home, or space. It usually involves significant changes, such as improving the use or appearance of space by moving walls, adding new paint, laying down a new floor, and so on.

Seller: The owner of a property who is selling it.

Selling agent (or buyer's agent): The realtor representing the buyer or tenant. (It is admittedly confusing that this person is called the *selling* agent, when it's the buyer they are working for.)

Selling brokerage (or cooperating brokerage): The brokerage representing the buyer or tenant.

Sign back: When one party signs the offer it has received and sends it back to the other party, usually having made changes to it.

Staging (or home staging): This is the process of preparing a property for sale, usually paying more attention to the interior, and can involve just de-cluttering and rearranging the existing furniture, or it can be more involved; for example, putting the seller's furniture and belongings into storage, and presenting an ideal image for potential buyers to consider by using rented furniture and props.

Tenant: A person or company who is paying the owner (landlord) for the right to use a property or space.

TREB: The acronym for the Toronto Real Estate Board (www.torontoreal estateboard.com).

About the Author

Claude Boiron is the co-author of *Commercial Real Estate Investing in Canada: The Complete Reference for Real Estate Investors and Professionals* (John Wiley & Sons Canada, Ltd., 2008). A broker with Coldwell Banker Terrequity Realty, he has transacted deals ranging from couples purchasing their first homes to complex commercial deals involving many millions of dollars, to residential, commercial, and industrial rentals. Boiron teaches a course entitled "Commercial Real Estate Investing" at the University of Toronto's School of Continuing Studies, a series of residential-focused courses at York University, and he has been retained by real estate brokers to teach 10-week courses entitled "Real Estate Sales Training" to their salespeople. He is often quoted by national newspaper journalists and is sought after for television appearances and various workshops, seminars, and webinars.

As a realtor, investor, landlord, and land developer who splits his time between residential and commercial real estate, Boiron is a rarity and a generalist who focuses on deal-making over the whole spectrum, in an industry that has spawned corporately managed specialists in each real estate type and geographic area.

Index